LIKE
HIM

Front cover: *Behold the Prints in My Hands* copyright © J. Kirk Richards

Cover and interior design by Natalie Brown
Art direction by Margaret L. Weber
Cover design copyright © 2021 by Covenant Communications, Inc.

Published by Covenant Communications, Inc.
American Fork, Utah

Printed in the United States

First Printing: October 2021

30 29 28 27 26 25 24 23 22 21   10 9 8 7 6 5 4 3 2 1

ISBN 978-1-52442-023-9

LIKE
HIM

*A Thoughtful,
Intentional Pursuit to
Becoming As Christ Is*

TABLE OF CONTENTS

Peace Be Unto You, GREGORY MORTENSON

FOREWORD

MICHELLE McCULLOUGH

I have often pondered Jesus's spending forty days and forty nights in fasting and prayer. We know the devil's temptations were an important part of Christ's growth and enlightenment toward godliness, but since He was alone, we know only a small portion of what happened in those days away from His disciples and historians.

What came as a result of His forty days and forty nights (among other things)? We read in Luke that Jesus returned to Galilee and then went to Nazareth, where He stood to read scripture. It was customary to do so in that day, but in this instance, He read about the coming of a Messiah and then told the people in the room that they were witnessing what had been prophesied for hundreds of years. They didn't understand and even questioned, "Is this not Joseph's son?" This group of people who were at church to learn about the coming of the Savior didn't believe Him when they saw Him.

To the people in the Church who didn't understand when Jesus said He was a fulfillment of all they had read—I get that. Without His suffering in Gethsemane and His death on the cross, it's hard to make His life and ministry make sense.

That Jesus once lived, loved, taught, and served has provided me an important portion of my testimony. That He died and rose again is my hope and my joy and the rock of my testimony. When I wander away from Him, His Atonement assures me that it is possible to turn back and His arms will be "stretched out still" (Isaiah 5:25) *every time*.

He seeks to help me grow without guilt and with a love that ignites my desire to want to do better for myself and for those around me. He comforts me, strengthens me, and brings me peace in times of heartache and trial. John said it best when he said, "Greater love hath no man than this, that a man lay down his life for his friends" (John 15:13). He did that for me, and He did that for you! Because of Him, I can be forgiven of my sins and shortcomings and I can have eternal life with our Heavenly Parents. He paid a debt I can never repay.

And while I may never make sense of all of it, this I know: eternal life is the goal. Jesus said, "I am the way, the truth and the life" (John 14: 6). It is through the Savior that eternal life is possible, and yet, while He was on the Earth, He didn't teach people how to die and enjoy eternity—He taught them how to *live*. His example provides a pattern of attributes that can help us be the kind of people we need to be here and in eternity.

As I read through the chapters in this book, many written by friends and people I have followed through the years (because of their love for and testimony of the Savior), I made a list of the twelve traits they wrote about. Each chapter provides insights into these attributes of Christ that can help us live peacefully, joyfully, and intentionally as we prepare to meet God and see Jesus Christ again.

As we examine our current temporal lives, there is likely room for improvement. I can see areas I have developed and areas I still need to work on. Truthfully and humbly, I can also see a trait or two I have really struggled with and, despite my efforts, have additional room to improve. His invitation to "come, follow me" (Matthew 4:19) never expires.

While I can see how far I've come to be more like the Savior over my decades on this earth, I can also see how far I need to go and how much more I can do to become more like Him. Am I willing to make the sacrifice of my time and my pride so I can get the promised blessings of what comes after?

It can be easy to look at this list and think, *I will never measure up. My weaknesses are too great, my efforts too meager,* and then ultimately think, *I will never be "perfected in him,"* as Moroni invited.

It took me decades of feeling uncomfortable with Moroni's invitation to come

"You are good enough and you are loved,

but that does not mean you are yet complete . . .

Only with His divine help can we progress towards becoming like Him."

—Scott D. Whiting

("Become like Him," Ensign, *Nov. 2020)*

to an important conclusion: I cannot be made perfect on my own. The ability to do it comes through the distinction "in him." I will never be perfect or celestial until I draw close enough to the Savior that I can access His Atonement and become like Him. But more than that, I cannot be made perfect until I can take advantage of every aspect of the Atonement—even down to the resurrection of my body and spirit to a perfect state. If we look closely, we will notice that when Christ is speaking to His followers during His mortal ministry, in Matthew 5:48, He says, "Be ye therefore perfect, even as your Father which is in heaven is perfect." Our Father was already perfect in thought, word, deed, and body. Jesus didn't consider Himself perfect until after He performed the Atonement and was resurrected to receive His perfect body. When He visited the Nephites, He said, "Therefore I would that ye should be perfect, even as I, or your Father who is in heaven is perfect" (3 Nephi 12:48).

Perfection comes after, and we have a whole lot of living to do to prepare us for that reunion and resurrection and culmination of all our efforts.

Doing this work to become like the Savior will have moments of insecurity and maybe even darkness, but as we persist, we are promised the light and love that can come only from a loving Savior who has already paid the price for us and now simply waits for us to have committed agency to come unto Him.

His patience will continue. His unity with God and His steadfastness with us will continue. With hope and diligence, He will continue to lead by example and show that there is room for us to grow and room for us in His charity and love. As we study and follow His example of obedience, brotherly kindness, and faith, we, too, can gain divine knowledge, patience, temperance, and virtue now that will help us achieve godliness eternally. Any sacrifice of time, be it forty days or even forty minutes learning and emulating His attributes, will prepare us for whatever comes next.

Dive in and enjoy. Whether you hop from one attribute to another based on

The Grateful Leper, Sarah Richards Samuelson

what you want to develop next or you read from cover to cover, may you hear the loving voice of the Savior leading you along, saying, "I am the light; I have set an example for you" (3 Nephi 18:16), and may you experience His hopeful promise, "Your joy shall be full" (3 Nephi 28:10).

Worlds without Number, ROSE DATOC DALL

GODLINESS

We Are All Divine

ALYSSA EDWARDS

The idea of another human manifesting the attribute of godliness seems difficult to conceptualize. When I think of other Christlike attributes, I can quickly attach them to another person. My mother is the perfect example of love, and my father, forgiveness; my sisters manifest virtue, temperance, and knowledge. I have struggled in navigating godliness because I have connected it only with the Savior. However, as I have spent more time studying and understanding this attribute, I have realized it is the sum of all the attributes—and even more importantly, we are all godly.

Claiming that every person is godly is bold. I recognize that not all of our actions are godlike, and perhaps the words we speak do not always match those of Deity, but I genuinely believe that due to our nature as children of godly Parents, we have godliness within us. Let me attempt to illustrate my thoughts.

A few months back, on the way home from work, I made a stop at the post office to drop off some packages. The purchasing line was short, so I decided to wait so I could also buy stamps. The postal worker and I made small talk. Midconversation, she paused, leaned in slightly, and stared intently into my eyes. A few seconds passed, and then she asked, "By chance, are you an Edwards? I am certain I have seen your eyes before." I lit up and replied that I was an Edwards (of which I am very proud). She replied that Marci had to be my mother. This stranger in the Lehi city post office was correct; Marci is, indeed, my mom. The postal worker was able to draw this conclusion simply because I have my mother's eyes.

I often wonder if our heavenly DNA works like our earthly DNA. Not only do I have physical characteristics of my earthly parents, but I also have different personality traits and attributes from them. If we inherit traits from our earthly parents, could it be that we have also inherited traits from our Heavenly Mother and Father? I truly believe what is taught in Genesis: "God created man in his own image, in the image of God created he him; male and female created he them" (Genesis 1:27). I imagine if we have a similar outer likeness, then our inner composition is rather homogenous as well.

How does one come to understand this attribute, which is so expansive and yet so personal? President Russell M. Nelson, speaking to members of the Tabernacle Choir, whom he said purely exemplify Christlike attributes, stated, "Godliness characterizes each of you who truly loves the Lord." The first step is to recognize that our human nature and godliness can coexist. Perfection does not create godliness. Rather, continual efforts and the power of

the Atonement allow access to the godliness inherent within us. My gratitude runs deep knowing there is not a certain grade or level that I must attain before I can acquire godliness if I am consistently working toward becoming more like God.

After we truly come to the knowledge that godliness does not mean perfection, we must understand our identity. If we do not understand our divinity, then godliness will seem absolutely far-fetched. Our divine (or godly) nature is not simply knowing where we came from; it is also acknowledging where we are going and how we are going to get there. Recognizing divine worth is not a passive action; it is a decision we must make consistently.

Peter illustrated godliness. This noble man was a fisherman by trade but made the decision to leave behind his nets and boat to follow the Savior. He, along with the other Apostles, witnessed miracle after miracle and continually gleaned teachings from Jesus Himself. But Peter did something that no other Apostle even attempted. He

"I have realized
Godliness is the sum
of all the attributes—
and even more
importantly, we are
all godly."

performed an act that had been done only by Jesus: Peter walked on water. Upon seeing Jesus do the impossible, Peter implored that the Savior call upon him to do the same. Peter had to have had a deep understanding and knowledge of his divine identity to even ask to perform something so unfeasible. The Savior beckoned Peter to come, and he did. He walked. Peter was a sinner. He had doubts, fears, and questions, but all of those can mingle with godliness and still allow a person to perform the most outrageous and amazing feats.

We may not be gods, but we are god-like. Just as having my mother's eyes does not make me my mom but makes me like her, we have traits of our Heavenly Parents that make us like Them. None of us has to manifest perfection in order to tap into our godliness. It is already there. That being said, we must trust in our Heavenly Parents, trust in our divinity, and know that we were created to be godly.

Leave Your Nets, ROSE DATOC DALL

Creation of Eve, J. KIRK RICHARDS

GODLINESS

To Be Like God

D. KELLY OGDEN

When asked, "Why are we here on Earth? What is our purpose?," we often answer, "We are here on Earth to get back to God's presence." To that response, my wife usually replies: "If that is our ultimate objective—to return to God's presence—why did we even leave His presence in the first place?"

Our more profoundly significant purpose is actually to *become like God.* If we become like our Father and our Savior, the place will take care of itself—we will be qualified to be in Their presence forever.

The first man our Father placed on planet Earth was Adam. Another name for Adam in the scriptures is Michael, and in Hebrew, that alternate name is mi-ca-el, which literally means "one who is like God."

Becoming like God should be the supreme goal of every one of Heavenly Father's children. The Beloved Apostle recorded the Savior's words from His great intercessory prayer, "And this is life eternal, that they might know thee the only true God, and Jesus Christ" (John 17:3). Our eternal life is bound up in coming to know Them—not just to know *about* Them but to know Them personally and to develop Their Godlike attributes. We must become celestial before we can inherit the celestial kingdom.

Godliness, then, is our all-inclusive purpose here on earth. One of the supernal titles in our Topical Guide is "Man, Potential to Become like Heavenly Father." The word man in the scriptures is a generic term meaning "human being" and refers to both male and female; for example, Doctrine and Covenants 20:18 states that God "created man, male and female,

"*Godliness,
then, is our all-inclusive
purpose here on earth.*"

after his own image and in his own likeness." On the doctrine of potential deification of Heavenly Father's children (also described as divinization or *theosis*), see the Church's Gospel Topic Essay, "Becoming Like God" (https://www.churchofjesuschrist.org/study/manual/gospel-topics-essays/becoming-like-god?lang=eng); Andrew C. Skinner, *To Become Like God—Witnesses of Our Divine Potential,* (Salt Lake City: Deseret Book, 2016). So, in mortality, we are in the process of acquiring godliness, learning the difference between good and evil and learning to choose the good, to become as the Gods (see Alma 12:31; Moses 4:11, 28).

While we are struggling through our earthly probation, John the Beloved noted: "It doth not yet appear what we shall be: but we know that, when he shall appear, we shall be like him" (1 John 3:2). More than three hundred years later, on the other side of the world, Moroni echoed the same doctrine: "all who are true followers of his Son, Jesus Christ . . . may become the sons [and daughters] of God; that when he shall appear we shall be like him, for we shall see him as he is; . . . that we may be purified even as he is pure" (Moroni 7:48).

Godliness, then, is the process of becoming like the Gods—our Heavenly Parents, our Savior, and the Holy Spirit—attaining, gradually and eventually, all the noble attributes They possess. The Apostle Paul wrote that in this lifelong pursuit, "we may lead a quiet and peaceable life in all godliness" (1 Timothy 2:2), having a determination, as Moroni added, to show a "strong faith and a firm mind in every form of godliness" (Moroni 7:30). The Prophet Joseph Smith taught that our effort to acquire godliness is a gradual, long-term process: "When you climb up a ladder, you must begin at the bottom, and ascend step by step, until you arrive at the top; and so it is with the principles of the gospel—you must begin with the first, and go on until you learn all the principles of exaltation. But it will be a great while after you have passed through the veil before you will have learned them. It is not all to be comprehended in this world; it will be a great work to learn our salvation and exaltation even beyond the grave" (*History of the Church* 6:306–7).

And Elder Bruce R. McConkie cautioned against toxic perfectionism, the drive to accomplish it all here and now: "You don't have to live a life that's truer than true. You don't have to have an excessive zeal that becomes fanatical and becomes unbalancing. What you have to do is stay in the mainstream of the Church and live as upright and decent people live in the Church—keeping the commandments, . . . loving the Lord, staying on the straight and narrow path. If you're on that path when death comes . . . you'll never fall off from it, and for all practical purposes, your calling and election is made sure" ("The Probationary Test of Mortality," address given at University of Utah, Jan. 10, 1982, 11).

The scriptures describe in considerable detail what constitutes "every form of godliness" that Moroni referred to—the character traits enumerated in this book and perfectly exemplified by Jesus Christ during His mortal ministry. The Lord's chief apostle asked, "What manner of persons ought ye to be in all holy conversation and godliness?" (2 Peter 3:11). Peter answered his own question by elaborating on the godly attributes that prepare us to be partakers of the divine nature: faith, diligence, virtue, knowledge, temperance, patience, brotherly kindness, and charity (2 Peter 1:3–7). Modern revelation urges our acquisition of similar godly character traits (D&C 4:6). These exalting characteristics could all be subsumed under the attribute godliness.

These qualities of godliness are depicted magnificently in God's holy temples. There we can learn the most elevated teachings of the eternal plan of salvation; there we make the essential covenants and receive the necessary ordinances that lead to exaltation in the celestial kingdom. The Lord has declared that "in the ordinances thereof, the power of godliness is manifest. And without the ordinances thereof, and the authority of the priesthood, the power of godliness is not manifest unto men in the flesh" (D&C 84:20–21).

We learn principles of godliness in the house of the Lord, carry that knowledge and understanding into our own houses, and there model in our families what it is to be like our heavenly Exemplars. This "education probation" enables us to obtain a high degree of godliness and continue to our "exaltation and glory in all things, as hath been sealed upon [our] heads, which glory shall be a fulness and a continuation of the seeds forever and ever"—that is, perpetual family throughout eternity. The Lord describes those who achieve this exalted state: "Then shall they be gods, because they have no end; . . . then shall they be above all, because all things are subject unto them. Then shall they be gods, because they have all power." We subsequently read the glorious reprise of John's ancient declaration: "This is eternal lives—to know the only wise and true God, and Jesus Christ" (D&C 132:20, 24). Learning and living godliness ultimately leads us to "the high calling of God" (Philippians 3:14).

Christus, J. KIRK RICHARDS

HOPE

Hope through Christ

G. SHELDON MARTIN

For quite a while, I thought *hope* and *faith* were synonyms; although there may not be a need to separate the concepts entirely, faith in Christ is an attribute that gives us confidence and trust in the unknown and the unseen, almost one step at a time, while hope in Christ is an attribute that can pull us through trials, difficult times, and even despair because we have an expectation that Christ has ensured a positive outcome. Faith engages us in the battle today, and hope reminds us the war is won.

"Hope is the confident expectation of and longing for the promised blessings of righteousness. The scriptures often speak of hope as anticipation of eternal life through faith in Jesus Christ" (www.churchofjesuschrist.org/study/manual/gospel-topics/hope). As Elder Dieter F. Uchtdorf taught, "Hope is not knowledge, but rather the abiding trust that the Lord will fulfill His promise to us. It is confidence that if we live according to God's laws and the words of His prophets now, we will receive desired blessings in the future. It is believing and expecting that our prayers will be answered. It is manifest in confidence, optimism, enthusiasm, and patient perseverance" ("The Infinite Power of Hope," Ensign, Nov. 2008).

Jesus Christ taught, "I am not alone, because the Father is with me. These things I have spoken unto you, that in me ye might have peace. In the world ye shall have tribulation: but be of good cheer; I have overcome the world" (John 16:32–33).

In that scripture, the Lord connects my hope and peace with His triumph over the world. At times, I live life with an attitude of, "I am trying to be good; shouldn't the Lord take away this challenge?"; whereas, it may be more effective to say, "Because I live in world with these challenges, I find hope that He has overcome what I am going through and I can overcome it too."

To go even further, President James E. Faust taught, "Hope is trust in God's promises, faith that if we act now, the desired blessings will be fulfilled in the future" ("Hope: An Anchor of the Soul," *Ensign*, Nov. 1999). I love the concept that I can root my hope in God's promises and in His ability to fulfill them in the future. With that solid foundation, I can have faith enough to act today. I don't need to see the result today. I just need to trust and have confidence that God will do His part.

Hope is so important when we are dealing with the tests of this life. We all experience heartache, trials, growth, and difficulty. At times, despair is defined as the complete loss or absence of hope. This darkness says there is nothing ahead. Despair is an emotion that debilitates the human spirit.

I have spent much of my career working with individuals in despair, and I have discovered vast differences in God's hope and Satan's despair. Despair is nothing I would want anyone to experience, but there is a great deal we can learn from it.

Despair is often born of fear rather than love—fear of shame, fear of failure, fear of punishment, fear of disapproval or disappointment. This can happen when we misunderstand what the Lord expects of us, and it can lead us to look "beyond the mark" (Jacob 4:14)—causing us to set expectations for ourselves beyond what the Lord has set and to torment ourselves unnecessarily when we don't meet them.

Though despair can come in differing degrees and for differing reasons, I have seen people get so lost in their fear and hopelessness that they cannot even see a reason to continue living. They get so lost in Satan's message that they can't dig themselves out of their failure or his telling them no one cares about them, so no matter how hard they try, they will meet only disapproval . . . so what's the point. Choosing to end it all is one of the most difficult decisions people in despair make, and it is one of the most

"Hope in Christ is an attribute that can pull us through trials, difficult times, and even despair because we have an expectation that Christ has ensured a positive outcome."

difficult decisions their loved ones have to deal with afterward. Sitting with a family after a death by suicide is among the most sacred, sensitive spaces I have ever been. In these situations of heartache and complexity, the family and friends often ask, "What could I have done differently?" and "Do I let my own despair defeat me?"

In speaking to these questions, Elder Dale G. Renlund taught, "This is not your fault. . . . Saying things like, 'How could my child have done this?' is also not very helpful because even you, as the loving parent, don't know enough to judge. . . . Leave that to God. I think that the right things are to know that your child now, in the spirit world, can progress. I believe that in the vast majority of cases we'll find that these individuals have lived heroic lives and that that suicide will not be a defining characteristic of their eternities" ("To Parents Who Have Lost a Child by Suicide," https://www.churchofjesuschrist.org/study/manual/videos/to-parents-who-have-lost-a-child-by-suicide?lang=eng).

When we realize there are circumstances beyond our control, we can focus on what we do have control over. This is where hitting the mark Jacob talked about in the Book of Mormon comes in. We must do what we are capable of and know that God will accept our best offering, no matter how great or small it is. When we accept our own capabilities, we will recognize God's acceptance as well. In those moments, we will feel His love, which will bring us hope. Hope born of God's love leads us down the path of obedience, covenants, and repentance.

Elder Jeffrey R. Holland, the ever-hopeful Apostle, expressed the reality of God's reach deep into despair and His ability to pull us out into the light of His love: "However late you think you are, however many chances you think you have missed, however many mistakes you feel you have made or talents you think you don't have, or however far from home and family and God you feel you have traveled, I testify that you have not traveled beyond the reach of divine love. It is not possible for you to sink lower than the infinite light of Christ's Atonement shines" ("The Laborers in the Vineyard," *Ensign*, May 2012).

Jesus Christ is, in fact, the hope of Israel and the rock of our salvation. Nephi taught, "Ye must press forward with a steadfastness in Christ, having a perfect brightness of hope, and a love of God and of all men" (2 Nephi 31:20). We do not deepen our hope in Christ by focusing on what we do but by focusing on what He did. The Atonement of Jesus Christ becomes the anchor of our souls. When we waver, stagger, and are tossed to and fro, we can find hope in the fact that He stands still and in the fact that He has already triumphed over all.

Raising of Lazarus, J. KIRK RICHARDS

HOPE

The Sandwiched Commandment
That Gives Us All Hope

TONI SORENSON

The Psalmist urged readers to "hope thou in God," and then he used a poetic phrase we should all commit to memory. He called God "the health of my countenance" (Psalm 42:11). Picture someone with a healthy countenance . . . someone who smiles through tears, who is resilient in the face of despair. That person has hope. Jesus exemplified hope. When Lazarus died and his sisters grieved him, Mary, overcome with sorrow, stayed in the house, but Martha hurried to greet Jesus, saying, "Whatsoever thou wilt ask of God, God will give it thee" (John 11:22).

That's hope borne of faith (Hebrews 11:1).

When they came to the cave where Lazarus's corpse was buried, Jesus taught a lesson on the power of pure hope: He "lifted up his eyes, and said, Father, I thank thee that thou hast heard me. . . . Thou hearest me always" (John 11:41–42).

Jesus thanked God for the miracle *before* the miracle occurred.

He could do that because He had hope, not just out of desire but out of belief in the goodness of God (see Jeremiah 29:11).

The recipe for obtaining that kind of hope is in the scriptures, smack-dab in the middle, between the greatest of all commandments and the one "like unto it" (Matthew 22:39). It's the mandate we tend to skip over. Here's the hierarchy: to love God first and then ourselves and our neighbors second. The scriptures repeat this commandment multiple times because it's so important (Leviticus 19:18; Matthew 19:19; Matthew 22:39; Mark 12:29–31; Luke 10:27; James 2:8).

Did Jesus love Himself? Did He practice self-compassion?

Without question.

Jesus showed us the way by being the way (see John 14:6). He loved the Father by keeping the Father's commandments (see John 14:15). He loved His neighbors by serving them (see Acts 10:38). And He loved Himself by remaining true to His spiritual identity (Luke 2:41–52). He stayed the course as He stayed about His Father's business, focusing His hope inwardly and not on the external things. For what's inside of us is eternal, but what's around us is temporal (2 Corinthians 4:16–18).

Because hope resides within us and we want to foster its growth, a critical part of our Heavenly Father's business is how we treat ourselves. I'm honored to work with the outcasts of the world, the souls whom society pushes to the edge and then abandons because they're addicted, afflicted, and undesirable. These are the souls who radiate hope. From them, I learn that when Jesus commanded that we forgive all those who have trespassed against us . . . that includes forgiving ourselves (Colossians 3:13). They believe He is our advocate because He understands what we go through. They have hope in the scripture that teaches us that Jesus took on the form of a servant that He might better understand the trials we humans endure (see Philippians 2:7).

Satan wants us to believe we are separate from God, because when we believe that, we despair. At the start of His ministry, Christ had an encounter with the devil, who took a hard swing, trying to steal the Savior's hope that He would be able to accomplish His mission. Satan attempted to cast doubt on the Savior's identity. "*If* thou be the Son of God . . ." (Matthew 4:6–8).

Never once did Christ doubt or deny His identity as a child of God (see 1 Corinthians 15:28). You and I have that same identity. Do we live true to it or downplay our divine power? Do we have hope that our lives have purpose and we have within us whatever it will take to accomplish our missions? While Jesus was never arrogant, He was never self-deprecating either. He lived in powerful humility, denying Himself

"Someone who smiles through tears, who is resilient in the face of despair. That person has hope. Jesus exemplified hope."

at times but never damaging Himself or destroying His intrinsic worth. That's how He remained hopeful.

I've learned that when we deflect compliments, we deny the goodness others see in us. When we insult ourselves because we sin or make mistakes, aren't we insulting the strength of God in us to change and improve? If we are going to practice self-compassion, then even in our most dire circumstances, we need to stop putting ourselves down and live with hope that God loves us, knows us, and has our backs. Pride has an ugly side that lies to us and tells us we're being humble when we fail to recognize and honor our God-given strengths and talents. Instead, we're humble when we remain hopeful, when we acknowledge, use, and give thanks for our godly attributes.

Jesus demonstrated self-compassion and exemplified how we should better love ourselves and live with hope. He prayed for spiritual and physical strength (see Matthew 6:9–13). He defended His personal values (see Matthew 21:12–13). When He was weary, He sought time alone to recover

and restore Himself (see Mark 7:24). He built a strong social support system (see Mark 3:14). He celebrated life's events and traditions (see John 2:1-11). He refused to be rushed (see John 11:4–6). He rejoiced in sharing the riches of God's grace with others (see Philippians 2:7). In everything He did, He gave thanks to the Father (see Colossians 3:17). First, He learned, and then He taught, receiving joy from giving back (see John 7:15). He did not disconnect from His emotions (see John 11:35). He lived in a state of faith and gratitude (see John 11:38–44). He rejoiced (see Luke 10:21). He lived His truth and accepted His Father's grace (see John 1:14). He stayed aligned with His priorities and said no when it was right to say no (see John 6:26–27; see also Matthew 16:23).

One of the most hopeful people I've known was an elderly woman named Clara, a grandmother in a string of foster homes that dotted my youth. Clara was bedridden but kind and hopeful even on her worst days. The "health of her countenance" relied on the health of her internal hope. Her service wasn't just reserved for those she telephoned daily to cheer. She held back a share for herself. She spoke gently to her legs when they failed her, she asked me to rub her fingers when they ached, and once, when others had forgotten her birthday, she made a paper crown to celebrate herself.

I asked her how she could be so happy in such sad circumstances.

She smiled. "My Savior loved me when my legs worked, and His love is big enough to hold me up even now when they don't."

Clara, like Jesus, had hope in things that to a worldly eye, do not exist. She had hope that the demise of her physical body had nothing to do with the condition of her spirit.

Jesus had hope that even before he'd called Lazarus from the dead, His Father had heard and answered His prayer.

They both had hope in God's big love.

Big enough for us to love God, others, and ourselves the way we've been commanded to love.

Big enough indeed.

Where Are Those Thine Accusers, ROSE DATOC DALL

BROTHERLY KINDNESS
God's Love—Our Joy
GLENN RAWSON

In the discussion of seemingly greater divine attributes, brotherly kindness is often overlooked, yet it is listed as one of those virtues that qualifies men for the work of the Almighty. The Savior is kind, considerate, and compassionate. Please consider the Lord's brotherly kindness in the following story and the outcome created thereby.

It was early in the morning when the Savior came into the temple to teach. A small group gathered to listen to Him when, suddenly, they were interrupted by a commotion. A group of men—scribes and Pharisees—approached the Savior, dragging a woman in obvious distress. They placed her strategically in their midst and, with a certain arrogance, declared, "Master, this woman was taken in adultery, in the very act. Now Moses in the law commanded us, that such should be stoned: but what sayest thou?" (John 8:4–5).

It was an ugly, ill-conceived trap. If Jesus said, "Stone her," He would incur the wrath of Rome and He would be contradicting His own teachings about forgiveness, love, and a higher law. On the other hand, if He said, "Release her; let her go," He would appear to be contradicting Moses, the revered lawgiver of Israel, and He would incur the wrath of the people. It would appear they had Him trapped, and no matter how He answered, He would condemn Himself.

Jesus didn't answer them. He considered the situation for a moment and then stooped and began writing on the ground as though He hadn't heard them. In doing so, He shifted the attention to Himself and away from the woman. The Jews gathered around Him and pressed for an answer.

While their attention was ruthlessly centered on Him, my heart goes out to the woman. For a moment, please step back and consider this woman. Whatever the circumstances of her guilt or innocence or the mitigating factors, I can imagine her—weeping, disheveled, and utterly humiliated and embarrassed. Guilty or not, she did not deserve such treatment.

Finally, the Savior rose and said, "He that is without sin among you, let him first cast a stone at her" (John 8:7), and then, without saying another word, He knelt again and resumed writing in the dust on the cobblestones.

His meaning was as sharp as a piercing arrow, and it penetrated their souls to the very core of their hardened sense of conscience. His voice must have thundered in their souls with godlike indignation. "You have no right to punish her when you are guilty of the same sins or worse!"

Convicted by their own guilt, they slunk off in order from the oldest to the youngest, leaving the woman. Jesus rose again and, seeing none but the woman, asked, "Woman, where are those thine accusers? hath no man condemned thee?" She answered, "No man, Lord" (John 8:10–11).

Please consider all that the Savior's reply entails: "Neither do I condemn thee," He said. "Go, and sin no more" (John 8:11). She was a sinner, as are we all. She was unworthy, and whether she deserved condemnation and punishment or not, it could not justly come from her accusers, and it would not come from Him. From Him, she received mercy, compassion, and kindness. If only we could have heard His voice and seen His face as He spoke to her. What effect did this encounter have on the woman taken in adultery? The scripture records, "And the woman glorified God from that hour, and believed on his name" (JST—John 8:11).

She was converted and became a disciple of Jesus from that moment forward. In the acts of divine providence, why is that story preserved? What are we to learn from it? Perhaps many things, but at least this: God is kind, and He is merciful to us in our mortal weaknesses and mistakes. They draw forth His grace and mercy, not His anger.

"When we receive that pure love from Christ and act on it, we are given the heavenly gift of pure love for Christ; His brotherly kindness for us fills us with love for others."

It is an essential element of our faith to know that the Father and the Savior love us with a pure, perfect, and everlasting love. It is our faith in that pure love and the kindness that follows that impels us to seek forgiveness and the very mercy the adulterous woman received. Our God is not the bitter, angry, vengeful being so often portrayed by misguided and often zealous Christians. John said simply, "God is love" (1 John 4:8). In "Lecture Third" of the *Lectures on Faith*, the Prophet Joseph Smith said, "Unless he [God] was merciful, and gracious, slow to anger, long-suffering, and full of goodness, such is the weakness of human nature, and so great the frailties and imperfections of men, that unless they believed that these excellencies existed in the divine character, the faith necessary to salvation could not exist; for doubt would take the place of faith, and those who know their weakness and liability to sin, would be in constant doubt of salvation" (*Lectures on Faith* [Salt Lake City: Deseret Book, 1985], Lecture Third, #20, 42). It is important to note that weakness and humility

elicit God's mercy (see Ether 12:27), while willful rebellion angers God.

God's love is not some nebulous, indefinable emotion. It is a real, discernible, spiritual gift imparted by the Holy Ghost (see Moroni 7:48). When we receive that pure love *from* Christ and act on it, we are given the heavenly gift of pure love *for* Christ; His brotherly kindness for us fills us with love for others. We treat all men as He does. After all, in the very day of judgment, what is it that will separate the sheep from the goats? It will be the kindness we manifest to others.

After standing in the presence of the Savior in the temple in vision, Elder Melvin J. Ballard described the Lord's tender kindness and then said, "The feeling that came to my heart then was: Oh! If I could live worthy, though it would require four-score years, so that in the end when I have finished I could go into His presence and receive the feeling that I *then* had in His presence, I would give everything that I am or ever hope to be!" (M. Russell Ballard, "The Blessings of Sacrifice," *Ensign*, May 1992).

Annointed One, ROSE DATOC DALL

If anyone reading this needs a kind friend and something to live for—something to work for—brotherly kindness is lasting happiness. God grant us the faith and love we need to be as He is—kind, merciful, and loving.

Zaccheus, J. KIRK RICHARDS

BROTHERLY KINDNESS
Looking Up!
S. MICHAEL WILCOX

It is always more desirable to view attributes of the soul than to describe them. That is the main truth inherent in the Father sending Jesus as a living image of Himself. All we are to become, we see in Jesus. He was the Father's Word, His message to His children, given in the visual life of His Son. Among the beauties of His character, His kindness was ever on display. Being kind with longsuffering tops the list of attributes in Paul's definition of charity. *Kindness* comes from an Old English word meaning "nation," implying all humanity is one and should be treated "brotherly." In Middle English, it evolved to mean "noble deeds," particularly those done with courtesy. Interestingly, we normally think of kindness as simple, everyday deeds of thoughtfulness. These stories show us the nobleness of simple kindness—Christ's brotherly kindness.

When I ponder the Savior's kindness, my mind leads me to the branches of a tree in Jericho, where a despised and marginalized man named Zacchaeus perched, desiring to merely see the Master. He's described as "little of stature"—not welcome among the "press" of more acceptable Jericho citizens lining the road (see Luke 19:3) Those two descriptions can be so emblematic of our society. Too often, we divide ourselves into the *press* and the *little of stature*. There are the popular, well-liked, favored, approved, similar-to-ourselves people, and then there are the disliked, obscure, dissimilar, inconspicuous, and unnoticed. People can be little of stature in another's eyes due to differences in ethnicity, race, physical appearance, economic state, cultural background, or personality. It is so easy when one feels part of the "press" to ignore, discount, even despise the little of stature. Here we must show brotherly kindness, especially in our fractured and divisive society, where even simple manners are drowned in the harsh and angry voices of dissention.

This diminutive man, unable to see over the heads of his fellow villagers who refuse to offer him a tiny spot on the road next to them, climbed a sycamore tree to watch Jesus pass. Of all the people in Jericho that day, who do you think Jesus chose to spend the day with—not just notice and speak to but be his guest? "And when Jesus came to the place, he looked up, and saw him, and said unto him, "Zacchaeus, make haste, and come down; for to day I must abide at thy house" (Luke 19:5).

How often I pray, "Father in Heaven, help me *look up* to see those in the sycamore tree!"

Zacchaeus then "came down, and received him joyfully" (verse 6). That is brotherly kindness! This whole story breathes brotherly kindness—it helped instill it in Zacchaeus as well as all of us who watch! Though Jesus was criticized for associating with a man the goodly "press" found unacceptable— "a sinner"—

Jesus knew this little friend "also is a son of Abraham . . . For the Son of man is come to seek and to save" (verses 9–10).

I think of Jesus's parable of the rich man and Lazarus. One of the striking qualities of the parable is the personalized addition of a name for the poor man: Lazarus. Beggar though he was, Lazarus had an identity. The rich man, interestingly, was not given a name, and I believe that was deliberate. Jesus asks us through the simple device of naming this beggar who hopes only for the crumbs from the rich man's table to see individual souls. We are so much more likely to show kindness when we perceive the humanity of others. Jesus seems to say to us, "This is Lazarus. He is not just a beggar. He deserves attention and kindness as a person, as a brother!"

There are no nameless masses, just brothers and sisters whose humanity we value. Jesus invites us to do noble deeds because we are one nation. And, of course, there is the ever-present kindness of His mercy and forgiveness, which He always immediately granted whenever anyone asked—from the

"There are no nameless masses, just brothers and sisters whose humanity we value. Jesus invites us to do noble deeds because we are one nation."

thief on the cross to Alma the Younger in his racked and harrowed agony. Christ would have us do likewise.

I cannot think of Zacchaeus and Lazarus—of brotherly kindness—without my mind turning to a poignant moment played out by a sixth-grade girl in the small town of Raymond, Alberta, Canada, who later became my wife. What she did as a young girl shows us what Christ emulates in the all-important attribute of brotherly kindness. Laurie wrote her experience for our children so they would fill their lives with "noble deeds." I conclude here with her words:

We called him James—never Jim or Jimmy. He lived on the edge of town in a dilapidated rundown house bursting with ragged dirty children. James's desk was right behind mine. The popular game of the time was called "James's Lice." James had immense buck teeth and was perpetually dirty year round. I never really saw through those layers of dirt until one bitterly cold January morning in the sixth grade. The nine o'clock bell had rung, and James's seat was empty until a mad blur came barreling into the room and flung open the cloak room doors. It was James. He tore open his coat, then quickly clutched it to him again. He had forgotten his shirt. How like James to forget his shirt in the dead of winter! He never wore a hat or mittens or even boots. But no shirt! So amid wild hysteria of guffawing sixth graders, he ran from the room back home.

An hour later, he returned, his face and ears white with the cold. It was then, for the first time, I saw his hands—deeply creased, raw, cracked, and bleeding from the cold. Mrs. Jones took him to the sink, washed his hands, and lathered them with lotion. His eyes met mine, and I saw James for the first time. He was mortified. He could laugh off our game of James's Lice, but to be cleaned and lathered in front of us was crushing, and I ached for him. Each succeeding day that the teacher worked with his hands, he shrank a little more.

I thought of the tiny lotion bottle in my pencil box and knew, somehow, I must give it to him. Then I tightened inside.

What if someone saw me? What if I were caught talking to James? I was careful that recess and waited for the others to go far into the field before I stopped James by the entryway and quickly shoved the lotion at him and said, "I want you to keep it so you won't have to go to the back there with the teacher anymore." He quietly examined it, put it in his pocket, and, without a word, turned to go. After taking a few steps, he pivoted and said softly, "Don't worry, Laurie, I won't tell anyone you gave it to me." He then left me—left me wanting to give, wanting to care—wanting.

As I knew her, Laurie never failed in her giving or her caring. And James helped her see with her Savior's eyes—eyes that always "looked up."

Fasting in the Wilderness, ROSE DATOC DALL

PATIENCE

A Bridge to Charity

GALE SEARS

Jesus Christ is patient. He learned patience in the great courts of heaven. For millennia, He watched His Father's children step onto the stage of mortality to try their wings on the flight of experience. As Jehovah, He tutored the imperious Israelites, time and again offering them a way out of wickedness. "For all this his anger is not turned away, but his hand is stretched out still" (Isaiah 9:12). Generation after generation, teaching, training, reaching out to His noble ones, only to watch David fall into sin, Solomon turn to strange gods, and His chosen people, miraculously released from Pharaoh's bondage, murmur over manna.

For hundreds of years, as the Shepherd of the Nephite nation, Christ warned of pride and the love of luxury only to watch a repeated course of doctrinal rejection and adoption of the natural man.

In His earthly sojourn, Jesus was patient with the insisting circumstance of mortality as He walked the dusty miles between Galilee and Jerusalem, dealt leniently with the foibles of the Twelve, and mercifully attended to the training of His followers, who were reluctant to acclimate to refined principles. With long-suffering, He attempted to lead the Pharisees and Sadducees away from their corrupted dogma to the vigor of eternal doctrines. The scriptures are replete with stories of the Lord's patience as He fasted forty days, freed the woman taken in adultery, stood mute before Herod, and bore the crucible of the cross for all of God's children.

Jesus Christ loves us, and "his hand is stretched out still" when we stray from the strait and narrow path. The metaphor of the hen gathering her chickens under her wings, as taught in the New Testament (see Matthew 23:37) and in the Book of Mormon is a clear illustration of the tender patience of Christ. In 3 Nephi 10:4–6 we read:

> O ye people of these great cities which have fallen, who are descendants of Jacob, yea, who are of the house of Israel, how oft have I gathered you as a hen gathereth her chickens under her wings, and have nourished you.
>
> And again, how oft would I have gathered you as a hen gathereth her chickens under her wings, yea, O ye people of the house of Israel, who have fallen; yea, O ye people of the house of Israel, ye that dwell at Jerusalem, as ye that have fallen; yea, how oft would I have gathered you as a hen gathereth her chickens, and ye would not.
>
> O ye house of Israel whom I have spared, how oft will I gather you as a hen gathereth her chickens under her wings, if ye will repent and return unto me with full purpose of heart.

Jesus Christ is patient as our Exemplar. He entreats us as children of God to learn this same patience for the salvation of our souls because it prepares us for heaven. We come to earth, we forget our wings, and we become entangled in earthly enticements and the lure of the natural man. If we desire to partake of the divine nature, we must diligently seek for and refine faith, virtue, knowledge, and self-control. When we attain these qualities, patience strengthens our spiritual stamina to endure to the end and to do it with godliness, brotherly kindness, and charity.

In 2 Peter 1:4–8, it says:

> Whereby are given unto us exceeding great and precious promises: that by these ye might be partakers of the divine nature, having escaped the corruption that is in the world through lust.
>
> And besides this, giving all diligence, add to your faith virtue; and to virtue knowledge;
>
> And to knowledge temperance; and to temperance patience; and to patience, godliness;

"With 'his hand stretched out still,' He forgives us when we stumble and promises that the end will be worth all our patient effort."

And to godliness brotherly kindness; and to brotherly kindness charity.

For if these things be in you, and abound, they make you that ye shall neither be barren nor unfruitful in the knowledge of our Lord Jesus Christ.

The Lord invites us to be patient with not only our fellow men but also with ourselves as we navigate the turbulent tribulations of life. As we patiently turn to the Lord in times of distress, we gain confidence in His ability to lift and heal, we deepen our trust in His timing, and we discover a perfect brightness of hope in His unceasing love.

Romans 5:3–5 says, "And not only so, but we glory in tribulations also: knowing that tribulation worketh patience; And patience, experience; and experience, hope: And hope maketh not ashamed; because the love of God is shed abroad in our hearts by the Holy Ghost which is given us."

Jesus Christ is patient. He stands at the finish line, beckoning us to run a good race.

With "his hand stretched out still," He forgives us when we stumble and promises that the end will be worth all our patient effort. In Hebrews 12:1, 2, Paul wrote, "Wherefore seeing we also are compassed about with so great a cloud of witnesses, let us lay aside every weight, and the sin which doth so easily beset us, and let us run with patience the race that is set before us, Looking unto Jesus the author and finisher of our faith; who for the joy that was set before him endured the cross, despising the shame, and is set down at the right hand of the throne of God."

Be still, my soul: The Lord is on thy side;
With patience bear thy cross of grief or pain.
Leave to thy God to order and provide;
In ev'ry change he faithful will remain.
Be still, my soul: Thy best, thy heav'nly Friend
Thru thorny ways leads to a joyful end.
("Be Still My Soul," *Hymns*, no. 124)

Master of Ocean, Earth, and Skies, ROSE DATOC DALL

Shepherd in the Spring III, J. KIRK RICHARDS

PATIENCE

The Patient Christ

SCOTT SORENSEN

Jesus Christ is a deeply relational Being. He continually walks a path that connects Him to His Heavenly Parents and to us. Notice His relational focus with the Father when He taught the Nephites, "And *my Father sent me* that I might be lifted up upon the cross." Then His attention shifts to His relationship with us: "And after that I had been lifted up upon the cross, that I might *draw all men unto me.*" Finally, Jesus connects us all to the Father: "That *as I have been lifted up by men even so should men be lifted up by the Fathe*r" (3 Nephi 27:14; emphasis added). To emphasize His relational character, Jesus likens Himself to the mother of an infant (see Isaiah 49:14–16), a good Samaritan (see Luke 10:29–37), a good Shepherd (see John 10:14), and even a protective mother hen (see Matthew 23:37).

To be this kind of infinite Being, Jesus has a deep, expansive character. Because patience is a core attribute of the character of Jesus Christ, patience must contribute to deep and fulfilling relationships with our Heavenly Parents, Jesus, ourselves, and others. What difference would it make in your relationships if you focused a little more energy and a little more prayer on being patient? Let us use two examples of Jesus to see what difference He made in the lives of people with whom He patiently interacted.

After the resurrected Jesus introduced Himself to a group of twenty-five hundred people in the Book of Mormon, He extended a profound invitation:

Arise and come forth unto me, that ye may thrust your hands into my side, and also that ye may feel the prints of the nails in my hands and in my feet, that ye may know that I am the God of Israel, and the God of the whole earth, and have been slain for the sins of the world.

And it came to pass that the multitude went forth, and thrust their hands into his side, and did feel the prints of the nails in his hands and in his feet; and this they did do, going forth one by one until they had all gone forth, and did see with their eyes and did feel with their hands, and did know of a surety and did bear record, that it was he, of whom it was written by the prophets, that should come (3 Nephi 11:14–15).

How long did it take for two thousand five hundred people to "one by one" have a personal experience with the Son of God? As Christ patiently connected with each person, what difference did it make in their lives? How were they different after this experience than they were before? In what ways did they treat others differently?

During the Last Supper, we get a somewhat similar story in the New Testament. There is a small detail in the scriptures as Jesus begins washing His Apostles' feet that is often overlooked. This detail makes a big difference in how Jesus desires to patiently connect with us one by one. John 13:4 explains, "He riseth from supper, and laid aside his garments; and took a towel, and girded himself." Stop and think of the imagery here. Bible scholar Thomas A. Wayment explained, "The *towel* spoken of here is a linen cloth, the type that was used by field workers as aprons. Jesus would have removed his tunic and cloak, and *thus he would have been dressed like a slave* in a loincloth or underclothing" ("The New Testament: A Translation for Latter-Day Saints," [Utah: Brigham Young University and Deseret Book Company, 2019], 192; emphasis added).

Can you picture the scene? Jesus intentionally dressed like a slave as He began to wash the feet of His Apostles. This powerful lesson would have been unmistakable to them. Imagine being Peter as he watched the Savior, dressed as a slave, wash his dirty feet—literally taking upon Himself Peter's filthiness. It is no wonder Peter reacted the way he did. What would that moment feel like? How would it feel to see your dirt and grime on the apron

*"How would
it feel to see your dirt and
grime on the apron Jesus wears
as He leaves you clean, pure,
and reborn?"*

Greatest in the Kingdom II, J. KIRK RICHARDS

Jesus wears as He leaves you clean, pure, and reborn? What would you know about the character of Jesus after this experience that you may not have fully realized before?

Now imagine being Peter as Jesus repeated this personal, kind, and loving act on the rest of the Twelve. I have often thought about how long this took. Did Jesus take one minute each, five minutes each, twenty minutes? Similar to the Nephite narrative, Jesus patiently served a group of people one by one. Although I don't know the exact hours and minutes, I do have an answer. This answer testifies of the patient Christ. The answer is *as long as it took*! That is what patience is! As long as we are willing to accept His invitation, Jesus will patiently work with us for *as long as it takes* for each of us to "see with [our] eyes . . . feel with [our] hands, and . . . know of a surety and . . . bear record, that it [is] he, of whom it was written by the prophets, that should come" (3 Nephi 11:15).

From the evidence of my own one-on-one experiences with the patient Christ, I believe Jesus wants to have an eternal relationship with me. I believe He is invested in this relationship with me for *as long as it takes*. And so it is with each of us; He will be with us *as long as it takes* "because of his loving kindness and his long-suffering towards the children of men" (1 Nephi 19:9).

Christ Tempted by Satan on the Temple Pinnacle, Study, ROSE DATOC DALL

TEMPERANCE

Living in the Pause

LAUREEN SIMPER

I've had the blessing of learning from some gifted clinical psychologists about the nature of the brain—particularly, the different cognitive functions of the limbic system and the frontal cortex. It's had profound spiritual implications on my better understanding the spiritual gift of temperance.

The limbic system of the brain is where our instincts reside, such as eating, breathing, and mating. The baser emotions of fear and anger, often referred to as the fight-or-flight response, come from the limbic system. In spiritual terms, the limbic system of the brain controls our natural man (see Mosiah 3:19).

The frontal cortex is where our humanity lies, where the difference between man and other animals is manifest. The development of the frontal cortex allows reason and principle to override instinct and emotion.

Because humans have a frontal cortex, there is what has been called a "pause" between an external stimulus and a person's response to that stimulus—in either a thought, a word, or a behavior. The frontal cortex serves as a filter for our brain, stopping us from acting on every unhealthy impulse our limbic system wants to act upon. In spiritual terms, the development of the frontal cortex is what allows us to tap into our divine nature we have inherited from our Heavenly Parents (see 2 Peter 1:4–7). And parenthetically speaking in a spiritual sense, the frontal cortex begins to develop in humans at age eight. Imagine that!

Our Heavenly Father has given us the capacity to learn, reason, and ultimately choose to change (aka repent) so we're not doomed to stay in the limited existence of merely reacting to outside stimulus. Because of the way our brains are created, we've been given the means to act rather than be acted upon (see 2 Nephi 2:13). It is here where temperance is born.

Jesus Christ was perfectly temperate. He had the infinite capacity to live within that millisecond pause between stimulus and response and, with perfect righteousness, override His human instincts of hurt, fear, or anger. His eons of perfect obedience to the Father gave Him the power to temper the baser instincts and, instead, choose to act on higher, holier principles of forgiveness, faith, and charity.

We fallen mortals will struggle to develop temperance—this mastery over our own instinctive existence—for two basic reasons: The first reason is our fallen natures themselves, which will create the resistance and opposition necessary for us to change and grow. Oh, how our feet of clay hold us down! The spirit may be willing, but our flesh, indeed, is weak (see Matthew 26:41). The limbic system was designed to keep us

alive, but inherent in that is the lifelong struggle between spirit and flesh.

Human nature (inherent limbic system) will always be in opposition to our divine nature (developing frontal cortex) because it's built into us. But there is a second reason we will struggle to bring forth that divine nature. The wickedness of the world at large provides an unhealthy nurturing environment in which to do it. To use Book of Mormon vernacular, the voices of the world—media, social media, government, even academia—"stir up" emotions. Sadly, this is often used to pit groups against each other, just as that strategy was used time and again in the Book of Mormon (see Alma 11:20; Helaman 6:21, 16:22; Mormon 4:5). Remember, emotions reside in the limbic system. Emotions, unchecked—*untempered*—make it difficult, if not impossible, to find our humanity—our divine nature—within the pause between the stimulus and the response.

We can take great hope in overcoming instinctive living where we merely react

"To develop temperance is to cultivate the ability to develop all other virtues. To develop temperance is to cultivate the ability to do the most intentional living our Father in Heaven hoped for us."

emotionally to our environment. The reason we can govern ourselves when we know correct principles is because *principles have the power to subject emotion.* This is temperance—the ability, enabled by the Spirit, to control our appetites, passions, and even ideas.

Temperance is at the heart of every other Christlike quality. Christ had the ability to fast for forty days because of His perfectly developed temperance. He had the ability to ignore Satan's temptations—when Christ was at His weakest—because of temperance. He had the ability to say exactly the correct and necessary thing in every situation because of temperance. His perfection turned that millisecond pause between stimulus and response into an eternity, allowing Him the power to make every single human choice intentionally.

Jesus Christ has the ability, because of His infinite atoning sacrifice, to widen that pause for us. To develop temperance is to cultivate the ability to develop all other virtues. To develop temperance is to cultivate the ability to do the most intentional living our Father in Heaven hoped for us. It requires more than reading or even studying doctrine; it requires metabolizing it—writing it on the fleshy tables of our hearts (see 2 Corinthians 3:3).

As God's word and will become ever more a part of us, we will know the correct principles sufficiently to govern ourselves, as the Savior governed Himself. It is temperance that will widen the pause between stimulus and response, allowing us to truly *choose* to be like Him.

Lord of the Vinyard, ROSE DATOC DALL

Behold the Prints in My Hands, J. KIRK RICHARDS

TEMPERANCE
The Limits on Meaningful Efforts
MEG JOHNSON

I was paralyzed when I was twenty-two years old, and since then, I've tried to figure out how to combine my personal limitations with my strengths to accomplish my purposes while I am here on earth. I recognize that Ether is right—when we allow our weaknesses to humble us and we accept what we can't change about ourselves and change what we can to become more like the Savior, we grow in ability. Even if our disabilities remain.

I can't "walk" the covenant path, but as I roll it, I've discovered that when I combine my weaknesses with my strengths and find someone to serve, I better discover my purpose in life.

Since being paralyzed, I've found others I can serve. In particular, I've started a pageant for little girls who use wheelchairs. I noticed a need for opportunities for girls to see themselves as beautiful, so I coordinated an annual two-day event with dozens of volunteers, participants, and performers.

We host our events in the late summer, and often, general conference is the next weekend.

One year after the pageant, I was listening to general conference for the attribute of the Savior I needed to work on. I felt prompted to focus on temperance.

I had just had a more stressful pageant and had lost my temper several times. I recognized that temperance was something I very much needed, but I didn't know how to obtain it.

Elder Scott D. Whiting said that any of us striving to become more like the Savior and grow in His attributes "will need to commit to exerting meaningful effort. These attributes won't come cheaply and suddenly, but through His grace they will come incrementally while endeavoring" ("Becoming like Him," *Ensign*, Nov. 2020).

"The Lord has said that we can lay hold upon every good gift, and the gift of temperance is something I have to continually seek."

What "meaningful effort" could I even exert? I pondered for several days about how I could possibly practice being temperate long enough to grow in it.

I think a lot when I drive, and I drive a lot. And one day as I was driving, I had a revelation. I could grow in temperance in the *car* if I drove the speed limit.

I immediately pushed on the brakes and slowed to sixty-nine miles per hour. The speed limit was sixty-five, but I thought that *for sure* I could never keep *that* commitment. I thought sixty-nine was slow enough. As it turns out, my speedometer was off, and my sixty-nine was sixty-five . . .

At first, it was very hard for me to drive sixty-nine miles per hour. The hardest was when other people were driving slower than I was (I never knew people actually drove that slow) and I couldn't pass them without causing other drivers to slow down. But it was in these and other difficult moments that I could feel myself growing in temperance.

I could tell I was becoming more controlled and temperate in my daily life, but the most telling experience happened during the next pageant.

During the first of the two events, while the participants were eating dessert and I was meeting with the judges, the entire venue reverberated with a loud, ear-piercing scream, followed by a glass-shattering, multi-object crash.

The judges and I were terrified, and one of them ran out of the room to help. She returned to explain that everything was okay. One of the volunteers had just tipped over a food cart near the elevators.

Even though I didn't let it show, I was fuming.

I finished the meeting and went to check on the volunteers. My plan was to verbally destroy the culprit. Why hadn't the volunteer been more careful? Why did she have to *scream?* That was the worst part! A mistake and a crash were understandable but not a loud, shrieking scream that echoed through the entire event.

As I pushed down the hallway, I remembered how often I'd sat behind a slow car in

the slow lane, wanting so badly to pass but knowing that if I did, I couldn't speed up enough to get around them before the other cars needed to use my lane. I remembered how often I had driven when I'd been late to a meeting but had still refused to allow myself to drive faster than sixty-nine. I remembered how often I had felt as if I were crawling when other cars flew by me.

I was feet away from turning the corner, and I could hear the volunteers picking up the crash site. It was the turning point, possibly the point of no return. I knew that if I rounded that corner, I would lose my temper. Even if I didn't say anything with my mouth, my face would say it all.

And this wasn't a time for me to speed. This was a time for me to turn around and drive the other way.

So I did.

And I never saw the commotion. I never saw which volunteer had tipped over the cart. I never saw who had screamed.

A couple of hours later, at the close of the event, one of the volunteers asked me if my first name was Grace.

"Um, no," I said. Most people ask me if my first name is Megan. It isn't. My full name is Margaret. But it's definitely not Grace.

"Oh," she said smiling. "I was sure that your first name was Grace and that your middle name was Under Fire." She went on. "I just can't believe how calm you are! I would be going crazy with such a big undertaking and so many people and so many problems to solve!"

I have been driving the speed limit ever since. The Lord has said that we can lay hold upon every good gift, and the gift of temperance is something I have to continually seek. I don't claim to be a temperate person, even now, many years of sixty-nine-miles-per-hour driving later, but I do believe I'm better than I was, and I'm hoping to improve behind every slow car.

Because of Him, TAUSHA SCHUMANN

Woman of Faith, ROSE DATOC DALL

VIRTUE

Who Touched Me?

SCOTT LIVINGSTON

She must have been beyond exhausted. Twelve years and she "was nothing bettered, but rather grew worse" (Mark 5:26). Her meager resources were spent. Multiple physicians had tried and failed to cure her of her painful, debilitating hemorrhage and, yet, nothing. He was her last hope.

Elder James E. Talmage sets the scene in his masterwork *Jesus the Christ*:

She worked her way through the crowd, and, approaching Jesus from behind, touched His robe; "For she said, If I may touch but his clothes I shall be whole." The effect was more than magical; immediately she felt the thrill of health throughout her body and knew that she had been healed of her affliction. Her object attained, the blessing she sought being now secured, she tried to escape notice, by hastily dropping back into the crowd. But her touch was not unheeded by the Lord. He turned to look over the throng and asked, "Who touched my clothes?" or as Luke puts it, "Who touched me?" As the people denied, the impetuous Peter speaking for himself and the others said: "Master, the multitude throng thee and press thee, and sayest thou, Who touched me?" But Jesus answered: "Somebody hath touched me: for I perceive that virtue is gone out of me" ([Salt Lake City: Deseret Book, 1982], 295).

Relief! Healing! Hope! Finally, she was healed, freed from the constant agony and shame such a condition imposed upon her. But how was it done? What had brought her long-sought-for miracle?

61

The visuals in this brief story are powerful. Jesus, accompanied by His disciples, is going to heal the dying daughter of Jairus, a leader of the local Galilean synagogue. Christ is literally surrounded or "thronged" by the numberless multitude. Some are followers. Others, merely curious. But regardless of their reasons for drawing near, *many* are touching Him. Peter's question is a fair one: "Master, the multitude throng thee and press thee, and sayest thou, Who touched me?" (Luke 8:45). But one among the crowd stood out. Her touching the hem of the Lord's robe was infused with faith.

Oh, to have been there for the moment when their eyes met, His and hers. The Master Healer and the one He had just healed. In the midst of a multitude, they were apart, separate from the rest. Clearly, she was fearful of a rebuke or condemnation: "And when the woman saw that she was not hid, she came trembling, and falling down before him, she declared unto him before all the people for what cause she had touched him, and how she was healed immediately" (Luke 8:47).

His gentle words in response were surely a balm to her sensitive soul: "And he said unto her, Daughter, be of good comfort: thy faith hath made thee whole; go in peace" (Luke 8:48).

What does this story mean for you and for me? How can we lay claim on His virtue, a word that means "divine strength or power"? Which of our hidden wounds awaits the Savior's binding up? What private heartbreak cries out to be "made whole"?

President Russell M. Nelson has taught, Do you remember the biblical story of the woman who suffered for 12 years with a debilitating problem? She exercised great faith in the Savior, exclaiming, "If I may touch but his clothes, I shall be whole. . . .

Many of us have cried out from the depths of our hearts a variation of this woman's words: "If I could spiritually stretch enough to draw the Savior's power into my life, I would know how to handle my

"How can we lay claim on His virtue, a word that means 'divine strength or power'? Which of our hidden wounds awaits the Savior's binding up? What private heartbreak cries out to be 'made whole'?"

heart-wrenching situation. I would know what to do. And I would have the power to do it."

When you reach up for the Lord's power in your life with the same intensity that a drowning person has when grasping and gasping for air, power from Jesus Christ will be yours. When the Savior knows you truly want to reach up to Him—when He can feel that the greatest desire of your heart is to draw His power into your life—you will be led by the Holy Ghost to know exactly what you should do.

When you spiritually stretch beyond anything you have ever done before, then His power will flow into you. ("Drawing the Power of Jesus Christ into Our Lives," *Ensign*, May 2017)

This divine characteristic of virtue is an "umbrella" attribute, meaning it weaves through and gives weight to many other Christlike attributes. Without God's virtue,

our hope of acquiring any of the Lord's divine attributes is vain. As President Nelson taught, to gain access to the Savior's power, we must approach Him in the same intense, even desperate state that this good woman approached Him—as if He is our last and only hope.

Isn't all that we do as developing disciples in some way tied to our need to be "made whole" through the virtue of God? Our prayers are pleadings for relief, for faith, for comfort. We search the scriptures for Christ, for assurance that He is able to enable us. The sacrament becomes our weekly pilgrimage to our personal "upper room" as we come seeking through a crust of bread and a sip of water to have the Good Samaritan bind up our wounds and "pour in oil" where there once was pain. Our ministering becomes what the prophet of God defines as "following your feelings to help someone else feel the love of the Savior in his or her life" (Sheri Dew, *Insights from a Prophet's Life: Russell M. Nelson* [Salt Lake City: Deseret Book,

Woman of Faith, ROSE DATOC DALL

2019], 349). And the temple, the house of the Lord? Surely it is a house of healing, where outstretched hands reach to touch the hem of heavenly help.

To receive the Savior's virtue is to receive Him. Just as this unnamed woman desperately sought divine healing after all other sources had failed her, so must we look to the only One who can bind up the brokenhearted. It begins with our outstretched hand of faith in the virtue of the Son of God. Our faith in Him will likewise make us whole.

Five Were Wise, MICHAEL MALM

VIRTUE

One Drop at a Time

STEPHANIE DIBB SORENSEN

From a young age, we develop a sense of right and wrong born from the light of Christ within us, and we mold our character and morality out of our experiences and choices. As I became a parent, I was more acutely aware that some of the choices I justified for myself were not necessarily the same things I would want for my children. This realization forced me to fine-tune my integrity and align my actions more precisely with my beliefs. As we practice intentional integrity, we magnify and deepen our personal virtue. Virtue is a synonym for power—a power that flows from righteousness. It was the source that Alma and the sons of Mosiah turned to when they found that "the preaching of the word had a . . . more powerful effect upon the minds of the people than the sword, . . . therefore Alma thought it was expedient that they should try the virtue of the word of God" (Alma 31:5).

How can we cultivate virtue in our own lives? Much like the lamp oil in the parable of the ten virgins (see Matthew 25:1–13), we can accumulate it drop by drop through consistent effort. Elder David A. Bednar explained, "As the wise virgins emphasized properly, each of us must 'buy for ourselves.' These inspired women were not describing a business transaction; rather, they were emphasizing our individual responsibility to keep our lamp of testimony burning and to obtain an ample supply of the oil of conversion. This precious oil is acquired one drop at a time—'line upon line [and] precept upon precept' (2 Nephi 28:30), patiently and persistently. No shortcut is available; no last-minute flurry of preparation is possible" ("Converted unto the Lord," *Ensign*, Nov. 2012). Every time we obey divine counsel, every time we resist temptation and choose light, every time we turn to the Savior for help, we add

"Virtue is a conglomerate attribute of integrity and goodness in all our choices."

to a wellspring of virtue. As we act in faith over and over again throughout our lives, seeking righteousness and reaching out to Jesus Christ, we stockpile virtue that can prepare us for times of need and sustain us by divine power.

In our Church vernacular, we often equate virtue only with sexual purity, but it is more than that; virtue is a conglomerate attribute of integrity and goodness in all our choices. However, chastity is an essential ingredient in our quest for virtue. The law of chastity demands that sexual activity be reserved for expression in marriage between a man and a woman and that it be exercised with fidelity and a reverence for sacred intimacy (see *General Handbook: Serving in The Church of Jesus Christ of Latter-day Saints*, 38.6.5). Elder David A. Bednar promised that "living the law of chastity invites some of the greatest blessings men and women can receive in mortality: appropriate spiritual confidence in the presence of family, friends, Church associates, and, ultimately, the Savior" ("We Believe in Being Chaste," *Ensign*, May

2013). The Lord testified that focusing our efforts on virtue—not just our actions but also our pure thoughts and words—can bring spiritual assurance: "Let virtue garnish thy thoughts unceasingly; then shall thy confidence wax strong in the presence of God" (D&C 121:45).

To strive for virtuous thoughts means avoiding salacious or degrading content that can darken our minds, but it also means seeking out sources of light that bring us closer to our God. What we choose to consume affects our spiritual capacity. The Lord Himself declared, "And if your eye be single to my glory, your whole bodies shall be filled with light, and there shall be no darkness in you; and that body which is filled with light comprehendeth all things. Therefore, sanctify yourselves that your minds become single to God" (D&C 88:67–68).

Once, my teen son was going through a dark time, and we had a conversation about the music he was listening to. He began to replace it with other music that allowed more light to enter into his mind. He had the humility to identify what parts of his life were blocking his access to the Spirit of God and His light. This effort led to feeling better about himself and the way he saw the world and those around him. Just as the scriptures promised, he felt himself grow in his confidence before God. Elder Marion G. Romney taught, "I can think of no blessings to be more fervently desired than those promised to the pure and the virtuous. Jesus spoke of specific rewards for different virtues but reserved the greatest, so it seems to me, for the pure in heart, 'for they,' said he, 'shall see God' (Matt. 5:8). And not only shall they see the Lord, but they shall feel at home in his presence" ("Trust in the Lord," *Ensign*, May 1979).

Because virtue is true godly power, the adversary fears it, fights it, and tries to counterfeit it. He perpetuates the lie that power comes from money, secular intellect, prestige, control, popularity or fame, appearance and seduction, and many other sources that bring worldly recognition but, ultimately, no spiritual

substance. Alternatively, virtue increases our worthiness and confidence before Heavenly Father; this leads to a greater sense of self-approval and self-respect. Contrary to the fleeting and fickle approval of the world, this confidence can be lasting and unwavering. Satan's counterfeits for power can garner temporary attention, but virtue makes one praiseworthy. Power that flows from righteousness increases our ability to influence others for good in important and eternal ways: "If there is anything virtuous, lovely, of good report, or praiseworthy, we seek after these things" (thirteenth Article of Faith). Virtue brings something beautiful into our lives, a light that invites the countenance of Christ (see Alma 5:14).

In her landmark talk, "A Return to Virtue," Sister Elaine Dalton declared, "Virtue begins in the heart and in the mind. It is nurtured in the home. It is the accumulation of thousands of small decisions and actions. *Virtue* is a word we don't hear often in today's society, but the

Latin root word *virtus* means 'strength.' Virtuous women and men possess a quiet dignity and inner strength. They are confident because they are worthy to receive and be guided by the Holy Ghost" (*Ensign*, Nov. 2008). Since we are not always strong, this accumulation of virtue will necessarily include a process of consistent and intentional repentance, and we can be regularly cleansed through the Atonement of Jesus Christ. Whenever I feel powerless or weak, if I turn to Him in prayer, study, and repentance, I grow in hope and light. When I try to increasingly focus my behavior on His example, I feel stronger. As we each seek for and practice virtue in thought, word, and deed, we can confidently draw upon the Savior's power and receive His assurance.

Christ Round Portrait, ROSE DATOC DALL

LOVE & CHARITY
A Heart Softened
HEATHER B. MOORE

And charity suffereth long, and is kind, and envieth not, and is not puffed up,

seeketh not her own, is not easily provoked, thinketh no evil, and rejoiceth not

in iniquity but rejoiceth in the truth, beareth all things, believeth all things,

hopeth all things, endureth all things.

—MORONI 7:45

By the time Moroni records his father's—Mormon's—words about charity, Mormon is already deceased. Yet his words live on and continue to teach in a significant way. The words *charity* and *love* are closely related and are often interchangeable. Just as Mormon teaches, "Charity is the pure love of Christ," and in addition, charity "endureth forever." A beautiful promise associated with possessing love and charity assures us, "Whoso is found possessed of it at the last day, it shall be *well with him*" (Moroni 7:47; emphasis added).

How do we access this charity? Showing Christlike love through our actions and words toward our loved ones will help them feel what it is for God to love them. We're counseled to show increased love even if we have disagreements (see D&C 121:43). Our actions of long-suffering, gentleness, meekness, and love unfeigned will bring us closer to emanating charity (v. 41).

And how do we dig deeper to find love toward others, even those who have become a burr in our side? How do we love our enemies, bless those who curse us, do good to those who hate us, and pray for those who despitefully use us, and persecute us? (See Matthew 5:44.)

Forgiveness and prayer are essential components in this process. President James E. Faust counseled, "Only as we rid ourselves of hatred and bitterness can the Lord put comfort into our hearts" ("The Healing Power of Forgiveness," *Ensign*, May 2007). What if we add to our prayers for a week or two those who have hurt us? Eventually, our hearts become softened toward them as we think of the pain and distress they might be experiencing in their own lives. As we are praying for our enemy, we are also sharing our burden with the Lord. We have been invited to do exactly this: "Come unto me, all ye that labour and are heavy laden, and I will give you rest. Take my yoke upon you, . . . For my yoke is easy, and my burden is light" (Matthew 11:28–30).

If praying for those who curse us and use us can ease our burdens and bring more peace into our lives, praying can also soften our hearts and fill us with love and goodwill. Yet, the concept of loving our neighbors, loving our enemies, and loving our families still might seem a lofty ideal. We have a Supreme example in our Savior, who

paved the way during His life upon the earth. There was not one person He turned away and not one person He shirked from teaching. He prayed for us *all*, regardless of gender, station in life, cultural belief, or religious persuasion. He prayed for those who sought forgiveness, and He prayed for those who didn't. He prayed for His Apostles, as well as for those who shouted, "Crucify him, crucify him," on the last day of His life (Luke 23:21).

Emotions at this injustice might war inside our human hearts; yet somehow, Christ was able to see beyond the terrifying events that would end His earthly life. In this way, He demonstrated the virtue of real charity. Elder Marvin J. Ashton said, "Real charity is not something you give away; it is something that you acquire and make a part of yourself. And when the virtue of charity becomes implanted in your heart, you are never the same again" ("The Tongue Can Be a Sharp Sword," *Ensign*, May 1992).

Emulating the Savior will certainly take us a lifetime of work, but when we understand what it takes to have day-to-day

"If praying
for those who curse us
and use us can ease our
burdens and bring more
peace into our lives,
praying can also soften our
hearts and fill us with love
and goodwill."

Loaves and Fishes, ROSE DATOC DALL

charity, we come to realize that we can begin this work this very moment. Beyond the elementary or vague to-do lists that always seem out of reach, Elder Ashton continued with this in-depth guidance: "Perhaps the greatest charity comes when we are kind to each other, when we don't judge or categorize someone else, when we simply give each other the benefit of the doubt or remain quiet. Charity is accepting someone's differences, weaknesses, and shortcomings; having patience with someone who has let us down; or resisting the impulse to become offended when someone doesn't handle something the way we might have hoped. Charity is refusing to take advantage of another's weakness and being willing to forgive someone who has hurt us" (Marvin J. Ashton, "The Tongue Can Be a Sharp Sword").

With this counsel in mind, we begin to see a clearer picture of how we might already be full of charity, or we may see areas where we can give more purposeful attention. And the next time we ponder Mormon's words penned by his son, we can gain our own personal insight into how developing charity will keep us on "the right hand of God" (Helaman 3:30).

Let us match our prayers to Moroni's plea: "Pray unto the Father with all the energy of heart, that ye may be filled with this love, which he hath bestowed upon all who are true followers of his Son, Jesus Christ; that ye may become the sons [and daughters] of God; that when he shall appear we shall be like him, for we shall see him as he is; that we may have this hope; that we may be purified even as he is pure. Amen" (Moroni 7:48).

And a Little Child Shall Lead Them, MICHAEL MALM

LOVE & CHARITY
Doing All Things for Love
JACK R. CHRISTIANSON

For about thirty years, I had the opportunity to help take care of a mentally and physically handicapped man named Dana Wilson. Almost every Friday or Saturday, he and I went grocery shopping. Each week, with little variation, we bought the same exact items. We spent many hours shooting three-point basketball shots at the institute of religion. Most days, Dana visited his many friends at the university adjacent to the institute. He often walked from office to office, watering plants and hunting for the "best" chocolate on people's desks. He was not well-kept physically. He didn't like to shave, wash, or brush his few teeth. He loved his Jack Russell Terrier, Dori, more than his life. They spent seventeen-plus years together. He also loved Primary Children's Hospital in Salt Lake City, Utah. He spent much time there as a child. As a result, each year for over a decade, he raised money and gathered gifts for the sick children by performing an Elvis Presley Christmas Concert. It was wildly successful, and those who loved Dana supported it immensely.

In November 2020, Dana passed away from the effects of COVID-19. As we gathered at his graveside for a brief service, I was humbled and brought to tears by the number of people who had braved the cold in order to pay their respects to this kind, gentle man. His rough and unkempt appearance was now gone. All that remained was his love for others and their love for him. As I stood to speak, two of Dana's daily statements came to my mind: "You know I love you, don't you?" and "Thank you for being my friend." Dana was love! He was charity! He exemplified the Bible Dictionary's definition of charity: "The highest, noblest, strongest kind of love, not merely affection; the pure love of Christ. It is never used to denote alms or

"If we are going to
be true disciples of Christ,
we are going to have
to learn how to pray with all the
energy of our hearts so we can be
filled with love & charity for all of
Heavenly Father's children!
Including ourselves!"

deeds, although it may be a prompting motive." This kind of love "never faileth"! And "it endureth forever"! (Moroni 7:46–47; see also 1 Corinthians 13:8).

The Prophet Joseph Smith taught, "Love is one of the chief characteristics of Deity, and ought to be manifested by those who aspire to be the sons of God. A man filled with the love of God, is not content with blessing his family alone, but ranges through the whole world, anxious to bless the whole human race" (*History of the Church,* 4:227).

The Savior of the World taught us that "faith, hope, charity and love, with an eye single to the glory of God, qualify [us] for [His] work" (D&C 4:5). Love and charity are what really matter in this life! Moroni counseled us to "pray unto the Father with all the energy of heart, that you may be filled with this love, which he hath bestowed upon all who are true followers of his Son, Jesus Christ" (Moroni 7:48). If we are going to be true disciples of Christ, we are going to have to learn how to pray with all the energy of our hearts so we can be filled with love and charity for all of Heavenly Father's children!

Including ourselves! We must learn to do all that we do for love! There can be no other motives but love!

"Charity is the pure love of Christ" (Moroni 7:47). It is His love for us and our love for Him! (See 1 Nephi 19:9; Ether 12:33–34.) Praying for love and charity must become a central part of our prayer and worship. Then we will see others as well as ourselves the way God sees us. Then we will see that what the Apostle John taught was true: "God is love" (1 John 4:16). We can then realize that all people, even the Dana Wilsons of the world, or especially the Dana Wilsons, are precious in the eyes of the Lord and should be treated with utmost dignity, charity, and love. Then the words of Elder Marvin J. Ashton, a former member of the Quorum of the Twelve Apostles, can sink deep into our hearts and help us become "true disciples" of Jesus Christ. Elder Ashton taught, quoting a discussion leader, "The best and most clear indicator that we are progressing spiritually and coming unto Christ, is the way we treat other people" ("The Tongue Can Be a Sharp Sword," *Ensign,*

May 1992). If we can be patient and continually strive for these two Christlike attributes and spiritual gifts, we will be better at doing all that we do for love and not for any other motive.

Having charity and doing things for love can become part of our daily lives. It is a simple concept, though it is not as simple to accomplish. A brief story related by Elder Vaughn J. Featherstone illustrates this concept. He told of a little boy who went to his mother's closet and took out her dress shoes, which were caked with dry mud from a recent storm. He washed the shoes and waxed and polished them. Then he waxed and polished them a second time, and finally, when they looked like new, he took them to his mother. She could hardly believe her eyes. She hugged him, kissed him, and went to her purse and took out a quarter, which she dropped into his hand. He looked at her with a deeply puzzled expression, put the quarter in his pocket, and returned the beautifully waxed and polished shoes to her closet. Several hours later, the mother went to change her clothes to go to the store. As she put on the freshly cleaned and shined shoes, she felt something down in the toe of one of them. She took the shoe off and shook it. A piece of paper fell into her upturned palm. As she opened the paper, a quarter fell to the floor. Then she read these words: "Mother, I did it for love" (see *The Light of Hope* [Salt Lake City: Deseret Book, 1979], 4–5. Also in Jack R. Christianson, *Unto the Least of These* [Salt Lake City: Bookcraft, 1993], 44–45).

As we pray for charity and love, as we seek to lift and bless others around us, may we do it all for love, as Christ did!

To Be with God, MICHAEL MALM

Daughter of Jairus, J. KIRK RICHARDS

DILIGENCE

"Let God Prevail"

SUSAN EASTON BLACK

Diligence is the steady application of letting the Lord prevail in our lives. In the October 2020 general conference, President Russell M. Nelson asked, "Are you willing to let God prevail in your life? Are you willing to let God be the most important influence in your life?" ("Let God Prevail," *Ensign*, Nov. 2020).

If your answer is affirmative, you will have many opportunities to be on God's errand, much like our Savior Jesus Christ always is. When a certain ruler said to Him, "My daughter is even now dead: but come, and lay thy hand upon her, and she shall live," Jesus arose and followed the man (Matthew 9:18–19). Although He had an urgent errand to complete, when the woman with the issue of blood touched Him, He paused to speak with her (Matthew 9:20–22). Why? For Jesus, His prayer was "not my will, but thine, be done" (Luke 22:42).

In a similar manner, as disciples of Jesus Christ, we oftentimes don't know when our diligence in heeding the will of God will send us on an errand from the Lord. What we do know is that we can commit ourselves through prayer to be diligent in seeking the Lord's will in our day. Why pray in this manner? If we fill our days with one thing after another, we miss opportunities to be diligent. Like drivers pushing the speed limit as they rush from home to the office and from the office to home, they create a predetermined straight path—but not necessarily the strait path that leads to eternal life. On the straight path, there is little room for inconvenience or patience.

Contrast the impatient drivers with the diligent disciples on the Lord's errand. With a prayer to begin their day and a prayer in their hearts throughout the day, these disciples make

"As disciples of
Jesus Christ, we oftentimes
don't know when our diligence
in heeding the will of God will
send us on an errand
from the Lord."

room to step away from personal agendas and let the Lord's will prevail. Take, for example, the actions of President M. Russell Ballard:

About six months before the death of Elder LeGrand Richards, one of his legs was amputated due to circulation problems. He was in great pain. As Elder Ballard was driving home from a stake conference and neared the intersection of Foothill Boulevard and 800 South, he received the impression, "Go see LeGrand Richards."

Elder Ballard drove straight to the home of Elder Richards's daughter Nona and knocked on the door. When Nona came to the door, she emotionally said, "Oh, Brother Ballard, my Daddy is something else!"

Elder Ballard replied, "Nona, the whole Church knows that your daddy is something else. Why did you say this?"

Nona replied, "Every time Daddy needs someone, the Lord sends someone to him."

Elder Ballard asked Nona, "What am I here for?" Nona led him to her father's room, where "this great apostle of the Lord lay in terrible pain." Elder Ballard said, "Elder Richards, it is Brother Ballard. Would you like me to give you a blessing?" Elder Richards nodded in agreement. Elder Ballard described "placing his hands on the head of LeGrand Richards as a spiritually refining experience." He then spoke these words: "LeGrand Richards, in the name of the Lord Jesus Christ, and by the authority of the holy priesthood vested in me, I lay my hands upon you to give you a blessing."

Of the words that followed, Elder Ballard said, "I testify and witness that the heavens were literally opened to my mind, and the

Lord spoke through me and blessed His servant. Before I concluded, Elder Richards was sleeping peacefully. As I left that sacred, special experience, I thanked the Lord for speaking to me at the red light on Foothill Boulevard and 800 South" ("Exercising Righteous Dominion," Bountiful Utah South Stake Conference, March 1, 1987. M. Russell Ballard Papers. Church History Library. Salt Lake City). The strait and narrow path is not a straight line. It is the covenant path that leads to eternal life, and "few there be that find it" (Matthew 7:14). By diligently letting the Lord prevail in our lives, we are on the covenant path. To the side of the path, we will find those who have stepped off for whatever reason. As we pause to help like Jesus did with the woman with the issue of blood, we will make a singular discovery: we are now farther down the path than we were before. That is the characteristic of diligence.

The Healing at Sundown, J. KIRK RICHARDS

Arise, Take up Thy Bed, J. KIRK RICHARDS

DILIGENCE

Jesus As a Model of Diligence

S. KENT BROWN

The gospels paint Jesus accurately as a fount of virtues that have made their way into the lives of uncounted followers. Let us take up the trait of diligence as it appears in two episodes from Jesus's ministry, one near the beginning and one at the end.

All are acquainted with the story of the widow in the village of Nain, how Jesus raised her only child, a son, from the dead. Behind this account lies a deep reservoir of diligence on Jesus's part. For starters, the day before, He was in Capernaum on the north shore of the Sea of Galilee, where, responding to a request to bring relief to a Roman centurion's servant, Jesus healed him from a distance. We recall that the centurion did not want Jesus to come to his house because it might cause problems of ritual cleanness for a Jewish man to come to a Gentile home (see Luke 7:1–10).

We next read that "the day after," Jesus "went into a city called Nain, and many of his disciples . . . and much people" followed Him (Luke 7:11). But they had to hurry. Why? Because traveling to Nain meant that a person covered almost thirty miles walking west and then south from Capernaum, most of it uphill. Jesus's journey would have required Him and His entourage to walk through much of the night to reach the town, whether they began very early in the morning, say about 2:00 a.m., or the day before, probably the prior afternoon. He and they had to reach Nain by mid-morning when the funeral procession came out of the gate to the cemetery. How, we might ask, does this story concern Jesus's diligence? Very directly.

In the first place, the distance is long. Jesus had to push the pace so He would not be late. And this fact uncovers another characteristic—love. He knew the desperate situation of the widow. Her only means of support was her son. With him dead, she had no income. To be sure, she could dip into her dowry that she had brought to her marriage. But as a poor person, the amount in her dowry would have been tiny. The story gives no hint that she had siblings onto whose generosity she could throw herself. Whatever belonged to her late husband, she could not inherit, only her children. But her one child was now gone. Her age (her son was twenty or so years old at his death) would have prevented her from offering herself as a wife to a brother of her husband to conceive another child who would inherit her first husband's property, an arrangement called Levirate marriage. Effectively, all doors were closed and locked for her. Remarkably, through his extraordinary powers of discernment (see Luke 5:22; 6:8; 11:17), Jesus knew her situation and took action. He came to help a woman He had never met, racing from one need (the centurion's sick servant) to another.

We can see in our mind's eye Jesus rapidly walking uphill toward the town gate to meet the funeral procession, His heart full of compassion for the grieving widow. When He came to the stretcher on which the dead body lay, He first addressed the widow: "Weep not." Then He pivoted to the bier. Grasping it firmly to stop it and hold it steady (that is the force of the verb *haptomai*), "he said, Young man, I say unto thee, Arise." We all know what happened next. Immediately, "he that was dead sat up, and began to speak" (Luke 7:13–15).

Here, in a moment, Jesus changed everything for the widow and her son. Gone from her was the looming uncertainty of how she would be able to get food and other necessities. Given to the son was the ability to see to the needs of his mother and to marry and bring children into their lives who would keep alive the name and memory of their grandmother and father. Importantly, except for a friend or two, the woman had no one on whom she could rely. No one outside the small town knew her or her son. But Jesus knew, and He acted to bring sweet relief to a woman who stood on the outer margins of society.

"He was all about helping people who could not help themselves. He was all about lifting those who could not lift themselves. And His Atonement was all about rescuing those who could not rescue themselves—all of us."

A second story brings us also to Jesus's diligence. We follow Him as He carried the cross piece to the place of crucifixion. During the prior week, He had taught daily in the Jerusalem temple, ratcheting up the intensity of His message in an effort to grab hearers' attention. What is striking about His journey to the place of execution is His almost desperate outreach to those who lined the path. He knew what was coming at them and their children forty years hence— the Roman legions that would bring the city to its knees. And worse.

Turning to the "great company of people, and of women, which also bewailed and lamented him," He fairly shouted out the words, "Daughters of Jerusalem, weep not for me, but weep for yourselves, and for your children." Why? Because "the days are coming," He said, "in the which they shall say, Blessed are the barren, and the wombs that never bare" (Luke 23:27–29). He knew that women, during a siege, would bear the burden of inevitable shortages in the city as they tried to scrounge food to feed their families. He knew they would bear the brunt of trying to escape with children from the enemy soldiers sweeping into the city and slaughtering anyone in their paths. He knew they would feel the physical anger of men who were looking to conquer their enemies by ravishing their women. Jesus knew, and He would not let go. To His last moment among these people, particularly the women, He kept up a litany of warning words. It would be the worst of times, a time of "great tribulation on the Jews . . . such as was not before sent upon Israel, of God, since the beginning of their kingdom" (Joseph Smith—Matthew 1:18).

These two accounts invite us to ask the question, Why did Jesus prize diligence? The counter question is also relevant: Why not? In response, He was all about helping people who could not help themselves. He was all about lifting those who could not lift themselves. And His Atonement was all about rescuing those who could not rescue themselves—all of us.

As a postscript, the Christians living in Jerusalem left the city before the Roman army arrived, their church leaders being

Surely He Hath Borne Our Griefs, J. KIRK RICHARDS

warned by revelation that they should leave town. They knew Jesus's prophecies of Jerusalem's fate and retreated to the town of Pella, which lay south of the Sea of Galilee on the east bank of the Jordan River. There they sat out the war untouched (see Eusebius, *Ecclesiastical History*, 3.5.3).

Source: This essay is modified from *The Testimony of Luke, The New Testament Commentary*, by S. Kent Brown © BYU Studies. Used with permission.

Among Thistle and Thorn, JENEDY PAIGE

FAITH

Faith in the Unknowing

CHRISTIE GARDINER

As a twelve-year-old girl camping in the mountains, I knew God was real. Looking up at the moon nestled between two pines in the cool night sky, and hearing the crackle of the fire nearby, I pulled my knees up to my chest. The knowing came over me as sure as anything I'd experienced. This wasn't a belief, a hope, or a wish. I grasped this insight with awe at what it was. It was more than faith; it was knowledge. God was real and loved me! Over the span of my life, I have at times communed with God. So have you. I have known my Savior has been with me, and I've heard Him. So have you. I have had glorious moments of absolute knowledge that I am not alone in this world—"signs from heaven" of His existence (Alma 32:17). So have you. These miraculous, interactive experiences in which we knew did not require our faith. As Alma said, "Now I ask, is this faith? Behold, I say unto you, Nay; for if a man knoweth a thing he hath no cause to believe, for he knoweth it" (Alma 32:18).

If we were to lay our lives out on a timeline, those bright spots of certain heavenly communion would be few in comparison to the number of moments lived. What is faith, then? Faith is what we forge when we choose to act based on inward spiritual understanding and conviction, without proof. Faith is what happens in the unknowing.

When we tell the story of the woman with the issue of blood in the Bible (see Matthew 9, Mark 5, Luke 8), we speak of her astonishing faith as she touched the hem of the Savior, knowing He would heal her. Our reverence for her act is deserved. Hers is a powerful story, and yet, are we not doing a disservice to this woman's experience when we assert that her faith was conceived in the second that she touched Christ's hem? While it was a courageous act inspired by faith, it was not the very instant in which her faith was built. She knew Christ could heal her; she was in His presence. She knew.

Upon the woman's touching His hem, Christ felt strength leave His body. When the Savior turned and saw the woman who had touched Him, she explained what had happened, telling him "all the truth" (Mark 5:33) of what she had been through for more than a decade. For twelve years, she had suffered with this isolating physical condition. Due to the times in which she lived, she would have been considered unclean and an outcast. She would have had very little human interaction and almost no physical touch. Twelve years of not being healed, spending all the money she had, seeing every doctor she could with no results—and ultimately, she chose Christ. She chose to believe she would be healed. She chose hope. She built reservoirs of faith within herself, nurturing the courage it would require as an "unclean" person and a woman to touch His hem—to act! She forged her faith alone so that in the moment she knew Christ was there, she would be prepared

to act on that faith. So powerful were the choices she made on her lonely road that when she finally saw Christ, she reached for Him with conviction.

Just as the woman with the issue of blood, our faith isn't born from choosing Christ in the moment of His presence— that is knowledge. Faith is choosing Him hundreds of times on our own, so when we do, with absolute knowledge, see Him, hear Him, or feel Him, we will have the courage to act from our storage of faith.

We experience much of our lives alone. Even the Savior Himself cried for heaven and felt forsaken. While we know Christ is with us all the time (see John 14:18), we don't always feel His physical presence. This isolation is an essential part of our Heavenly Parents' plan that allows us space in which we choose our own path. It is in these moments of often lonely choice that our faith is forged. Faith is choosing Christ and our Father and Mother in Heaven even in Their perceived absence. It is choosing Christ and living the plan He was willing to die for. We can come to understand that heaven's

"She chose to believe she would be healed. She chose hope. She built reservoirs of faith within herself, nurturing the courage it would require as an 'unclean' person and a woman to touch His hem—to act!"

silence is not evidence of our failure; rather, the silence is the very thing that will enable us to prove our faith with our works. For what good is faith without works (James 2:17)? What good would the faith of the woman with the issue of blood have been if she had not touched the robe, had she not had the courage to walk with Him when she had the chance? What good would the faith of any of us be without our action?

In the eons, will there ever be a time I physically walk with Christ? Just Him and me? I picture walking on a beach—mostly because beaches are my favorite of God's creations. There we are, walking side by side, in the purest of sibling love. Everything that used to matter to me is washed away by the healing tide of His Atonement.

I think of all the lonely times I've still chosen Christ. The times I've felt abandoned. The times I've been betrayed, misunderstood, maligned, mocked. The times living on earth has seemed impossible, with pandemics, terrorism, natural disasters, and wars, but also with the vicissitudes of everyday life. The times I've cried out for Him

and, in spite of the longing of my heart, have chosen Him in His seeming silence. Sometimes waiting mere seconds but sometimes years between loving interactions of assured communion with Him. And yet, looking back, each of those life-defining times of choice are the atoms that make up the matter of my faith. Those were the times I chose Him without knowledge, and "[my] faith [in choosing Him] hath made [me] whole" (Luke 8:48; see also Matthew 9:22, Mark 10:52). Because of those moments, my faith is not without works (see James 2:17). It is not dead. It lives!

Sitting here in my midlife, thinking of all that has been required of me in the past and all that surely lies ahead feels exhausting. But "I know that my redeemer liveth! . . . In my flesh shall I see God!" (Job 19:25–26). I would do it all again for the promise of that beach walk. I do it all now for the very hope of it. In my mind's eye, I see Him there, standing in the surf, His hand outstretched as the waves crash in, then slip back out. I'll meet you there, Jesus. Wait for me. I'll choose faith and meet you there.

The Invitation, JENEDY PAIGE

Faith as the Mustard Seed, ROSE DATOC DALL

FAITH
Faith to Move Mountains
HEIDI S. SWINTON

I grew up with a huge portrait of my great-great-great-grandmother hanging in our living room. She was regal in her countenance and wore a lovely lace mantilla over her hair. I knew she was important in the early days of the Church; she had attended the first meeting of the Female Relief Society in Nauvoo and served as the general Relief Society president in the early 1900s. She had received her endowment from the Prophet Joseph Smith and had been the matron of the Salt Lake Temple. But what I didn't realize until I was an adult was how important she was to me.

Bathsheba W. Smith joined the Church in Virginia, faced the persecutions of Missouri, and married the love of her life, George A. Smith. They settled in Nauvoo, where George was called as the youngest Apostle in the history of the Church, and the two became thoroughly engaged in the Restoration of the gospel. While George served several missions, Bathsheba hired workers to plaster the walls and finish the roof of their small home that she then decorated with her paintings and hand-stitched lace cloths and curtains. She lived true to the Lord's counsel in 1830: "Lay aside the things of this world, and seek for the things of a better" (D&C 25:10).

The journey to "better" times was not easy; like most Saints—then and now—she faced relentless hardship, disappointment, sickness, and death of loved ones.

In the bitter cold of February 1846, she, George, their two children, and five sister wives crossed the Mississippi in the first exodus from Nauvoo. They left behind the newly completed temple, their fields and orchards, their gardens, and their homes. Bathsheba wrote in her journal of her departure:

We left a comfortable home, the accumulation of four years of labor and thrift and took away with us only a few much-needed articles such as clothing, bedding and provisions. We left everything else behind for our enemies.

My last act in that precious spot was to tidy the rooms, sweep up the floor, and set the broom in its accustomed place behind the door. Then with emotions in my heart which I can not now pen and I strived to conceal, I gently closed the door and faced an unknown future, but I faced it with faith in God (Journal of Bathsheba W. Smith, in author's possession).

"Faith in God" is displayed in our willingness to follow Him. That was the key for my grandmother Bathsheba and hundreds more like her who have helped put down the roots of the Lord's Church in the latter-days. So many times when my life has taken a dramatic turn, I have thought of her, the waiting wagon, and the broom behind the door, and I have exerted faith to go forward. All of us, at some point, are asked to do the same. Every challenge, suffering, test, or trial in mortality is an opportunity to strengthen our faith in Jesus Christ, the Deliverer, the Author and Finisher of our faith. He has promised in the midst of what may seem the darkest day, "Let not your heart be troubled, neither let it be afraid" (John 14:27). If we are following Him, no matter the heartache or hardship, our faith in the "master of ocean and earth and skies" ("Master the Tempest Is Raging," *Hymns,* no. 105) will make the difference. We will press on with "a steadfastness in Christ" (2 Nephi 31:20). I have been there, and so have you.

Faith is heeding the Lord's call "to paths that we do not know." In the familiar anthem, we sing:

> *It may not be on the mountain height*
> *Or over the stormy sea*
> *It may not be at the battle's front*
> *My Lord will have need of me.*

"Faith in Jesus Christ prompts us to do things we otherwise might not do. Peter jumped over the side of the boat at the Lord's call to 'come,' and he walked on water."

But if, by a still, small voice he calls
To paths that I do not know,
I'll answer, dear Lord, with my hand
in thine:
I'll go where you want me to go.

("I'll Go Where You Want Me to
Go," *Hymns*, no. 270)

Said the Savior to His disciples, "If ye
have faith as a grain of mustard seed, ye shall
say unto this mountain, Remove hence to
yonder place; and it shall remove; and nothing shall be impossible unto you" (Matthew
17:20). I don't think He was talking about
rocks and earth as much as the weight we
carry on our shoulders. Often, they feel like
mountains piled on mountains. Did Bathsheba wring her hands when the call came
to cut a trail west? Did she murmur, "This is
a hard thing you ask," as Laman and Lem-
uel did, when they, too, were asked to leave
their homes and flee into the wilderness?
No, she squared her shoulders, and to the
mountains of doubt, disappointment, and
foreboding she said, "Move aside." And they

did. She put her faith in the Lord's promise:
"Fear not, little flock; . . . let earth and hell
combine against you, for if ye are built upon
my rock, they cannot prevail" (D&C 6:34).

Faith in Jesus Christ prompts us to do
things we otherwise might not do. Peter
jumped over the side of the boat at the
Lord's call to "come," and he walked on
water (see Matthew 14:28–29). Bathsheba
closed the door and went west. Both required the courage described in Proverbs
3:5–6: "Trust in the Lord with all thine
heart; and lean not to thine own understanding. . . . and he shall direct thy paths."
For Peter, the path was wind-swept waves
(see Matthew 14:28–29); for Bathsheba, it
was wind-swept plains. For us, in our wind-
swept, troubled times, the Lord whispers,
"Peace I leave with you, my peace I give
unto you" (John 14:27).

Faith centered in Jesus Christ leads to
exaltation. That's a sweeping statement, but
faith in Him, the King of Kings, is the first
and overarching principle of the gospel.
Faith prompts obedience, hope, charity,

love, virtue, honesty, compassion, and courage. Faith is cast as trust, confidence, and belief. It enables us to rise above our struggles, pains, and disappointments, to drop our nets, as did the Apostles of Jesus (see Matthew 4:19–20). and follow Him, whose work this is. "Be faithful in Christ," Mormon taught, that "the grace of God the Father whose throne is high in the heavens, and our Lord Jesus Christ, who sitteth on the right hand of his power . . . be, and abide with you forever" (Moroni 9:25–26).

Bathsheba tenderly loosed herself from the moorings of her home and comfort. Many times, so have I. The Apostle Paul calls the faith Bathsheba exhibited "press[ing] toward the mark for the prize of the high calling of God in Christ Jesus" (Philippians 3:13–14). Her resilience, her mettle and, yes, her faith in the Lord has given me strength to do the same, and He, the Son of the living God, has been there for me.

All Ye That Labor, J. KIRK RICHARDS

HUMILITY

Humility Is Strength

GANEL-LYN CONDIE

As we look at Jesus Christ's mortal ministry, we might possibly come to the conclusion that humility is strength. In a world of hashtags, these three words tell us not only about the King of Kings, but they also give His followers the secret compass to holiness. And that compass is humility.

Humility is an acknowledgment that our talents and abilities are gifts from God. It is not a sign of weakness, timidity, or fear; it is an indication that we know where our true strength lies. We can be both humble and fearless. We can be both humble and courageous. (https://www.churchofjesuschrist.org/study/manual/gospel-topics/humility)

No one would dare describe the Savior as timid, weak, or fearful. In fact, in the scriptures, we see Him as an example of the "greatest hits" of immense courage and power. Jesus not only walked on water, turned water to wine, fed the thousands, and healed the blind, but He also raised the dead to life! If any one of us mere mortals participated in such miraculous missionary work, we may be tempted to boast in our own power. Not Jesus. During His earthly mission, He testified that His strength came from total dependence upon His Father: "I can of mine own self do nothing. . . . I seek not mine own will, but the will of the Father which hath sent me" (John 5:30).

The topics of the gospel, the "what's" and "why's," fill Come, Follow Me lessons and general conference talks, leaving us as developing disciples to worry and wonder about the how as we cultivate the Christlike attribute of humility. Christ may be our sinless exemplar, but at least

"He was known
as prophet, healer,
priest, and Prince of
Peace. His motivation
wasn't about His glorified
titles but about glorifying
His Father's title in
all He did."

part of our adoration lies in the fact that He is not human-less. His example is accessible and inspiring for us, for "Jesus increased in wisdom and stature, and in favour with God and man" (Luke 2:52). We are invited to walk where Jesus walked, to step where He stepped along the path of humility.

Let's look at those steps and explore how they impact our own journey toward humility.

THE STEP OF STEWARDSHIP

Jesus seemed to grasp the concept of stewardship versus ownership at a young age. He understood that stewardships are opportunities to share our talents and gifts. They are about the offering, not the outcome. When He was twelve years old, "[Mary and Joseph] found him in the temple, sitting in the midst of the doctors, both hearing them, and asking them questions. And all that heard him were astonished at his understanding and answers. And when they saw him, they were amazed: . . . And he said unto them, How is it that ye sought me? wist ye not that I must be about my Father's business?" (Luke 2:46–49).

At this tender age, Jesus astonished and amazed the learned. Knowing He was about His Father's business, His life had a grander purpose than His simply being "teacher of the year." He was known as prophet, healer, priest, and Prince of Peace. His motivation wasn't about His glorified titles but about glorifying His Father's title in all He did.

Can we see our opportunities as stewardships instead of as ownerships? Often, we can't control what happens; we can only control what we get out of it. It is not as much about increasing the number of baptisms, likes on a social media post, or getting a raise at work. It is more about how we dedicate ourselves to serving the Father throughout our day.

Jesus taught in the temple because it was His Father's business. He wasn't trying to be the best salesman in the business; instead, He was glorifying the Boss of the business. So the next time you astonish the kids with a dinner they don't want or create a video to amaze your coworker who is getting a big promotion, remember that humility is found in celebrating and seeing all experiences as stewardship assignments. Then, win or lose or whether your kids make the choices you like or whether the video goes viral, the glory always goes to God.

The how of humility is found in the steps of stewardship.

THE STEP OF SERVICE

From the beginning of time, service and humility have seemed to go hand and hand. Recall that in the heavenly family council, Jesus humbly volunteered to serve His family. When the Father's plan was presented, Jesus said, "Here am I, send me" (Abraham 3:27.) From the beginning, the Savior put the needs of others before His own.

He forced no one to listen to His teachings or to be healed by His touch. The Messiah's successful service mission never led to becoming myopically self-focused. In fact, He ultimately gave the greatest, most wide-sweeping gift of all: His life.

Christ taught by example that humility is a byproduct of service. One of the most tender moments of His ministry came during His last days with the Apostles when He washed their feet. Elder Jeffrey R. Holland taught, "In New Testament times, people wore open sandals, walked on mostly dirt roads that accumulated the filth of beasts, and had only irregular access to bathing water. Their feet became very dirty, and washing another person's feet could have been a distasteful task. . . . This custom of hospitality was usually performed by the lowest level of servants" (*New Testament Student Manual* [Church Educational System manual, 2014], 242). Elder Holland tells us that during this final supper, "Christ quietly arose, girded himself as a slave or servant would, and knelt to wash the Apostles' feet" (See John 13:13–17) ("He Loved Them unto the End," *Ensign*, Nov. 1989, 25).

Today, the ancient practice of washing feet has been replaced with more ordinary opportunities to serve. We find it on the face of a beleaguered parent after a long night with a sick child. In the hands of an adult child wiping the forehead of a dying parent. In the arms of a neighbor hugging a grieving friend.

The how of humility is found in the steps of service.

For She Loved Much, J. KIRK RICHARDS

THE STEP OF SILENCE

One of the most difficult steps of humility may be this final one—the steep step of silence. Elder Neal A. Maxwell taught: "There can be dignity even in silence, as was the case when Jesus meekly stood, unjustly accused, before Pilate. Silence can be an expression of strength. Holding back can be the sign of great personal discipline" ("Meekness—A Dimension of True Discipleship," *Ensign*, March 1983).

But how is staying quiet a sign of strength?

Jesus counseled with the ignorant and the learned, the proud and the low. He had answers for every question and yet sat in silence to allow questions to be asked. Innocent of all wrongdoing, He, in the end, surrendered to His accusers and was humbly crucified on the cross alongside the truly guilty. He offered forgiveness to His mockers and abusers. It was in these moments of meekness that Jesus's glory shone brightest.

So why is it so hard for us to hold our tongue or extend love to our enemies?

Recently, a state politician and his family showed the how of humility when protestors arrived at their rural home, dissenting a decision he had made. The demonstrators were angry. Instead of showing hostility in return, the politician's family served the protestors warm plates of cookies. The sweet treats softened the activists' hearts, and the next day, newspapers reported the peaceful protest instead of hateful headlines.

To defend and protect feels like the natural response, especially when falsely attacked and accused. Humility-induced silence is a gift of grace, one we can pray for. Jesus knew who He was and that the accusations against Him were false, yet He maintained noble silence. Maybe the next time you find yourself being indicted, consider prayer and silence as a response. Turn to God. He, above anyone else, knows how it feels and how to succor you as you take the step of silence.

The how of humility is found in traveling along the path the Savior's steps show us—stepping forward in our own stewardships, service opportunities, and sacred silence: The Lord will strengthen us as we humble ourselves before Him. "God resisteth the proud,

Art Thou a King, J. KIRK RICHARDS

but giveth grace unto the humble. . . . Humble yourselves in the sight of the Lord, and he shall lift you up" (James 4:6, 10).

Thy Will Be Done, HOWARD LYON

HUMILITY

Humility: A Lifelong Quest

LLOYD D. NEWELL

It may not be an overstatement to say that the plan of salvation was set into motion by an act of humility. Before the world was created, when the Father said, "Whom shall I send?" (Abraham 3:27), two spirits volunteered. And what was the difference between the two? One was prideful, boasting, "Behold, here am I, send me, I will be thy son, and I will redeem all mankind, that one soul shall not be lost, and surely I will do it; wherefore give me thine honor." The other was humble, saying simply, "Father, thy will be done, and the glory be thine forever" (Moses 4:1–2).

Thus pride became the first distinguishing trait of Satan, while humility became the first distinguishing trait of Jesus Christ.

This struggle between pride and humility is older than the earth. And like the war in heaven that it sparked, the struggle continues today—including in our own hearts.

It doesn't help that the world in which we live is fiercely competitive—some would even say ruthless. The pressure to succeed, to get ahead, to win leads many people to become aggressive and dominating, proud and self-important. The sentiments of "Here am I" and "I will do it" and "Give me thine honor" that ultimately barred Lucifer from heaven can seep into our lives and lock our hearts to the blessings of eternal life. Pride is a barrier between who we are and who we can become. It imposes limits on our growth, because it declares, in the words of Korihor, that we succeed in life "according to the management of the creature" and that every one of us prospers according to our genius and strength (Alma 30:17). Pride cripples us by turning us away from the enabling power that could be ours through Jesus Christ.

Pride is animosity in action. It pits us against one another in competition and comparison. Whether we are looking down on others condescendingly or looking upward covetously, pride drives a wedge between us and our fellow beings. Our "vainness and foolishness" (see 2 Nephi 9:28–29) hinder us from finding true intimacy with our brothers and sisters, our fellow children of God.

But there is a different, better way to live. It is, in a word, humility.

Humility breaks down barriers—those that separate us from each other and from God. Humility unlocks our hearts, allowing the Savior to enter in and begin His healing work.

Humility is, in many ways, "the key of knowledge" (Luke 11:52). Lucifer, with all his cunning, "knew not the mind of God" (Moses 4:6)—not because he was unable but because he was unwilling. Humility liberates us from the confinement of our own constricted views and limited wisdom, opening our eyes to the Lord's higher thoughts and higher ways (see Isaiah 55:8–9).

True humility gives us hope for the future and helps us endure the difficult present. Those who are humble are less likely to lose hope when things go wrong or when they fall short, because they aren't depending on their own power to overcome such failures. They trust that the Lord's grace is sufficient to make weak things strong. The humble can always ask for help, and they don't insist on that help on their timetable. The humble have a sensitive conscience and are quick to repent. Often, this also makes them sympathetic toward the weaknesses of others and, therefore, quick to forgive.

The humble don't see other people as their competitors. Rather, they see God as the inexhaustible source of all good things, so they don't assume that good fortune for one person means less of it for themselves. Consequently, they are less likely to be resentful when a gift or blessing is given to someone else.

God loves all His children. But He does not force His love upon us. We must humbly receive it.

"*Humility breaks down barriers—those that separate us from each other and from God. Humility unlocks our hearts, allowing the Savior to enter in and begin His healing work.*"

Thread of Faith, HOWARD LYON

That creates a paradox for those who have come to believe that our skills, talents, or accomplishments are what earn people's love. If we acknowledge our weakness, our helplessness, our foolishness, won't God love us less? The truth is He already knows these things about us—our strengths and our weaknesses, our abilities and our deficiencies. Indeed, "the Lord God showeth us our weakness that we may know that it is by his grace, and his great condescensions unto the children of men, that we have power" (Jacob 4:7; see also Ether 12:27). If we humble ourselves before Him, the Lord will lead us by His loving hand (see D&C 112:10).

That may sound simple, but we all know it isn't easy. Humility is a lifelong quest. It is a choice we must continue to make throughout our lives. And interestingly, the more we work at it, the more we realize how much work it takes. But that, too, helps us to be more humble.

I know a man who taught religion at Brigham Young University for some fifty years. He is well educated, with a PhD from an elite university. He has studied and written much over these many decades. His academic vitae is lengthy and impressive. And yet, he said to me, "When I first arrived at BYU, I was quick with the answers to most questions. Over the decades, as I have learned and grown both spiritually and intellectually, I find myself more and more saying, 'I don't know; I'm not certain.' Some things, like my testimony and my convictions of the truthfulness of the restored gospel are stronger than ever. But on other things, I am less ready with a response, less quick to give the immediate answer, less inclined to pretend I know everything."

That is humility.

Weathering Autumn, ROSE DATOC DALL

KNOWLEDGE

Christ's Perfect Knowledge Is
Our Eternal Blessing

ANDREW C. SKINNER

One of the truly unique attributes of Jesus Christ, compared to all other inhabitants of this earth, is His all-encompassing knowledge. The Book of Mormon prophet Jacob declared, "O how great the holiness of our God! For he knoweth all things, and there is not anything save he knows it" (2 Nephi 9:20). This attribute is often called omniscience (from the Latin words *omni*, "all," and *scientia*, "knowledge"). Many other passages of Restoration scripture testify of this truth, leaving no doubt about its certainty (see 2 Nephi 2:24; Mormon 8:17; Moroni 7:22; D&C 127:2). God is infinite, eternal, endless, and perfect; so is His knowledge (see D&C 19:10; 20:17). When we speak of God in these or other passages, we mean both God the Father and His Son, Jesus Christ, who was God, the Great Jehovah, before He came to earth in mortality, and He remains so today (see Mosiah 3:5; D&C 29:11; 110:3–4). And we know, as Jesus Christ Himself testified, He and His Father are one (see John 17:11)—He is "one in the Father" (D&C 35:2) in terms of understanding, purpose, and knowledge.

Significantly, the Book of Mormon prophets Lehi and Moroni speak of God's omniscience in the context of the plan of redemption through Jesus Christ, the most important knowledge mortals can acquire. Lehi said, "All things have been done in the wisdom of him *who knoweth all things*. Adam fell that men might be; and men are, that they might have joy. And the Messiah cometh in the fulness of time, that he may redeem the children of men from the fall. And because that they are redeemed from the fall they have become free forever, knowing good from evil" (2 Nephi 2: 24–26; emphasis added). Note that the result

"We can rest assured that no miracle is beyond His ability to provide; no problem or issue we bring to Him is beyond His capacity to take care of in ways that best serve His work, which is to bring to pass our immortality and eternal life."

of God's knowledge was humankind's redemption through Christ (He knew the fall would happen and would require an Atonement), which led indirectly to our own knowledge of good and evil. Likewise, Moroni's witness was that because God, "*knowing all things*, being from everlasting to everlasting, . . . sent angels to minister unto the children of men, to make manifest concerning the coming of Christ; and in Christ there should come every good thing" (Moroni 7:22; emphasis added).

In both of these texts, we see that an aspect of God's omniscience is His foreknowledge of events. Jesus Christ certified that He possesses infinite foreknowledge: "All things are present before mine eyes" (D&C 38:2). This is corollary to a statement He made to Abraham millennia ago: "My name is Jehovah, and I know the end from the beginning" (Abraham 2:8). God knows He can and will bring to fruition all His intentions and purposes for humankind as well as all creation because of His infinite foreknowledge. As the ancient Church leader James stated, "Known unto God are all his works from the beginning of the world" (Acts 15:18).

Early on in this earth's temporal history, Jesus Christ demonstrated His awe-inspiring foreknowledge when He "showed Enoch all things, even unto the end of the world" (Moses 7:67). However, it should not be thought that God's foreknowledge of what will happen takes away humankind's choices or moral agency. Elder Neal A. Maxwell explained,

> For God to foresee is not to cause or even to desire a particular occurrence. . . . The actual determinations . . . are made by *us* mortals using *our* agency as to this or that course of action. For these determinations and decisions we are accountable. . . . Our agency is preserved . . . by the fact that as we approach a given moment we do not know what our response will be. Meanwhile, God has foreseen what we will do and has taken our decision into account (in composite with all others), so that

his purposes are not frustrated. . . . In a very real sense, all we need to know is that God knows all!" (*All These Things Shall Give Thee Experience* [Salt Lake: Deseret Book, 1979], 12–21).

Jesus Christ's divine omniscience also includes the ability to know the thoughts and intents of human souls. He told Joseph Smith, "There is none else save God that knowest thy thoughts and the intents of thy heart" (D&C 6:16). This stunning truth was known to Old Testament rulers and writers. To Solomon, King David made a fatherly appeal: "Solomon my son, know thou the God of thy father, and serve him with a perfect heart and with a willing mind: for the Lord searcheth all hearts, and understandeth the imaginations of the thoughts" (1 Chronicles 28:9). Indeed, the ancient Apostles understood that the Lord "knowest the hearts of all men" (Acts 1:24). And for what purposes? One of them is to act as a fair, merciful, and forgiving Lord and Judge. In further reporting Solomon's dedicatory prayer for the Jerusalem temple

after he became king, the Chronicler recorded Solomon's petition to God: "What prayer or what supplication soever shall be made [from] any man, or [from] all thy people Israel, . . . hear thou from heaven thy dwelling place, and forgive, and render unto every man according unto all his ways, whose heart thou knowest; (for only thou knowest the hearts of the children of men" (2 Chronicles 6:29–30).

Because Jesus Christ possesses all knowledge, we also know, by divine definition, that He is full of truth (see John 1:14), for "truth is *knowledge* of things as they are, and as they were, and as they are to come" (D&C 93:24; emphasis added). Jesus possesses "a fulness of truth, yea, even *all truth*" and designated Himself as the Spirit of truth (D&C 93:26; emphasis added). There is no truth He does not comprehend: scientific, historical, or philosophical.

Jesus Christ's omniscience is linked to His intelligence. He is the greatest, most intelligent of all our Heavenly Father's sons and daughters (see Abraham 3:19). Moreover, as Elder Maxwell again reminded us, Jesus Christ "is utterly incomparable in what He is, what He knows, what He has accomplished, and what He has experienced. . . . In intelligence and performance, He far surpasses the individual and the composite capacities and achievements of all who have lived, live now, and will yet live!" (see Abraham 3:19) ("O, Divine Redeemer," *Ensign*, Nov. 1981, 8).

It is a great blessing to know that our Lord is all-knowing and that not only is His knowledge infinite but also that "his understanding is infinite" (Psalm 147:5). We can trust Him completely. We can cultivate unrestrained faith in Him. We can rest assured that no miracle is beyond His ability to provide; no problem or issue we bring to Him is beyond His capacity to take care of in ways that best serve His work, which is to bring to pass our immortality and eternal life (see Moses 1:39). President Joseph Fielding Smith said, "The Lord is constantly using his knowledge in his work," (*Doctrines of Salvation*, 3 vols. Bruce R. McConkie compiler [Salt Lake City: Bookcraft, 1954], 1:10). Because

we understand that God is omniscient, possessing infinite understanding, we can and should, at His invitation, "come boldly unto the throne of grace, . . . obtain mercy, and find grace [defined as enabling power (Bible Dictionary, "Grace")] to help in time of need" (Hebrews 4:16).

Let Not Your Hearts Be Troubled, HOWARD LYON

KNOWLEDGE

Crisis to Faith to Knowledge

RACHELLE PACE CASTOR

I have a wing room in the upstairs loft of my home. It was created after a series of heartbreaks: we closed a business, lost a beloved house, and endured three subsequent moves all while attempting to stop a convicted pedophile that led to tables-turned deception and betrayal and left children even more vulnerable. My heart was in shreds.

At times overwhelmed with grief, I struggled with confusion, anxiety, and depression. Our apartment living meant no private area and no escape into nature. Working every waking hour to recover financially made it nearly impossible to find alone time. Scripture study was interrupted; prayers were shortened to accommodate work schedules; there was no rest from the chaos. Although my faith remained, my confidence was gone.

I knew restorative time was essential to transform trauma into strength. I continued to work toward more consistent scripture study, temple worship, and meditation. More than any time before, I needed heavenly guidance, yet it felt so far away.

Over several years, our financial circumstances improved, and heaven's idyllic timing showed up, leading us to a little place called Vineyard. The property was impossibly perfect. Our new home sat on a peninsula surrounded by a large pond overlooking endless acres of protected marshland, a lake in the distance, and mountains all around.

In the planning stages, I penciled in a room that would serve as a sort of sanctuary. I fully accepted it would remain empty until we could afford nonessentials. Even without furnishings, the room's bone structure was a natural haven. Along with being isolated from the rest of the house, the room's one window was precisely set to look out over our pond and frame

"We can find
quiet and rest as we
experience Zion's pure
knowledge, for it is all around us.
Close your eyes, breathe deeply,
and connect heart, mind, and
spirit as you grow wings
of light."

Mount Timpanogos. I planned to escape to my room often and watch as the sun, wind, and moonlight painted a thousand different faces on the water. Canadian geese would fly in by the hundreds, with rare glimpses of a blue heron or white crane. How could I wish for more?

Even so, the Lord could see that more was needed, and soon after we moved in, a financial windfall made it possible to add furnishings, drapes, art, and a mirror framed in a butterfly motif. Weeks of searching, purchasing, placing, arranging, and rearranging brought perfection. As I admired my now complete sanctuary with deep satisfaction, it dawned on me that everything the room requested had wings: birds, angels, butterflies; even the view from the window included an endless array of waterfowl. My room had known all along what it would become. I stood there in awe and unceremoniously named it in a whisper—"Welcome home, wing room."

Soon, I learned why I had felt inspired to create a place for stillness and rest. God had a plan. He knew there would be people, not a few, seeking that much-needed sanctuary. He could see that my own desperate need for solitude would manifest my compassion and call to those who needed the same. A friend in emotional crisis, a divorcing sister, a young woman betrayed, concerned parents needing to be near their anxiety-stricken college student, a son needing to heal. Many have come. Some for a night or two. Others for months. All have needed time to restore their tattered faith to a new perspective of enlightened certainty—to knowledge.

It wasn't long before I found *myself* needing time in my wing room to recover from broken ribs, damaged eyes, and an injured neck after an auto accident. I learned again how crucial quiet repose was after trauma. Stillness and rest were essential to be able to hear the uniquely personal counsel for healing and growth. I learned a new way of listening despite the endless pain and sleepless nights by homing into and recognizing God's voice. At times, my mind would take over; at other times, my emotions; and always, the physical pain seemed determined to shut me down, causing me to choose from a place of fear, habit, and instinct rather than wisdom. What I wanted was for my healing path to manifest from the perfect love of the Great Physician. My wing room's quiet privacy and beauty, along with the patterns of nature I observed through the window, taught me simple practices of how to establish equanimity.

The process seemed far too simple, but it worked. I would close my eyes, place my hand on my heart, and breathe as deeply as broken ribs would allow. Visualizing a bridge of light connecting heart and mind, it was as if a conduit from heaven would open with new ideas and options, untethering me from fear and pain so I could observe with all my senses unrestricted and tuned into truth. This ability to name, honor, and learn from my experience established a well-lit path to healing. Pain became my teacher. Recognizing and respecting my emotions led to responses anchored in free will and choice rather than reaction. It took weeks to learn how to access this wisdom and much longer to put a language to it and write about the process. Yet, now I know, as do many fellow sojourners.

My wing room has become that restful space, allowing myself and others time to move from crisis to faith to knowledge. The unexpected gift that has circled back is an up-close glimpse into the hearts of my precious guests as they process emotions brought on by difficult experiences and shape those experiences into gems of knowledge. There have been moments when "groanings which cannot be uttered" (Romans 8:26) have disseminated through the walls of that room. Occasionally, I have felt to knock gently and offer human contact to the anguished soul. More often, I've felt prompted to remain in another part of the house and stand in prayer, assisting my guest by holding them up, spirit to spirit, as they do alone the work of harrowing the holy ground of the heart. I have been given a tiny glimpse of knitting hearts as one, becoming a Zion people, and learning to rest.

Not One Shall Be Forgotten, NAOMI BROWN

And there shall be mine abode, and it shall be Zion, which shall come forth out of all the creations I have made; and for the space of a thousand years the earth shall rest (Moses 7:64).

You may not feel to design a wing room, nor is it necessary. However, you will have what God sees as needful for *your* healing and growth.

No matter how difficult the journey, deep the wound, or impossible the path, we can find quiet and rest as we experience Zion's pure knowledge, for it is all around us. Close your eyes, breathe deeply, and connect heart, mind, and spirit as you grow wings of light.

Renewal, JENEDY PAIGE

OBEDIENCE

Embracing the Unexpected

AL CARRAWAY

I was twenty-one years old, living in New York, when I was baptized into The Church of Jesus Christ of Latter-day Saints. And let me tell you, before all that happened, *life was good*. So when I learned that God is real and He is mine, I was elated. I honestly felt unstoppable in everything that followed, moving forward with the Creator of the entire universe on my side.

Life was good . . . until it wasn't.

Because, as it turns out, I'd never known such painful sacrifice and loss and loneliness *until* I joined the Church. I'd never known real pain, indescribable anguish—until I got baptized, I'd never struggled so long and so hard that my body literally ached. I began to experience times when I felt my desperate pleadings weren't heard or that my faith and my God were failing to protect me from the unwanted and the unexpected and the uncharted that I was consistently being called to wade through. I found myself screaming at God until I literally lost my voice, wondering where He was, if He even still cared about me or if He was even there at all. My life consistently fell into a rhythm of going from bad to worse to even worse. Where were these promised blessings of obedience we heard so much about? What if I really could live however I liked? Was His path always going to feel this heavy and lonely?

It would be so easy to quit, you know? To give up. To go back. Back to where twenty-one years of habits, tradition, contentment, and culture lay deep within my roots—within my *being*. To leave behind the trying times. I know very well the times when a person loses their voice, loses hope, loses strength. Those times that feel unheard, unanswered, unwanted, unfit, unworthy. Feeling lonely, lacking, tired. Times of wondering, wandering, and doubting, guessing, questioning, struggling, sinking, and sacrificing. Those times we feel our faith and our efforts are in vain as we move forward with no change. Those times when another day doesn't seem like another chance but another burden to bear, forcing us to use faith when we don't even know whether we have it. How easy it is to blame God and run away from His "supposed path" with what seems in the moment to be "supposed blessings" attached to "supposed requirements."

It would be easy to quit, but I know how worth it and possible and crucial it is to keep going in obedience. To *truly* live. And, *ahhhh,* what a life it is! We may not know the *what* or the *why,* but we do know the *Who.* A God who is good, even when our situation is not.

Remember God. His entire existence is to bring us to the better and make us better. Regardless of passing time, regardless of where we are on a certain path, and regardless of how crafty and powerfully subtle the

adversary is, these cannot take away from the reality that the purpose of God's *entire* existence is to lift us higher.

While Heavenly Father watched as His Only Begotten Son was mocked and spit on and falsely judged and murdered, the scriptures say, "It pleased the Lord to bruise him" (Isaiah 53:10). *Why?* Because there was, in fact, something *so much bigger* to come. Because God knows something we don't. *Something greater.*

So what if we've got it all backward? What if every step is the miracle?

When we see our seasons through, embrace the unexpected, and allow God to be God, *wow,* does life blossom! Every time I have yelled at Him, wondering where He is, I have stepped closer to *everything* I have now. The crying, complaining, and confusion all turned into the *best* things. My favorite things. And it pulls at my heart to imagine my life any differently. Everything I love the most stems from all that I was initially fighting against.

I think we forget that. I think we forget that the unexpected is God intervening. I

"When we see our seasons through, embrace the unexpected, and allow God to be God, wow, does life blossom!"

think we forget that we don't truly want things our way. I think we forget how *thrilling* it is to live by faith and obedience. To live as He asks and take heart in things not going how we want, take heart in our unexpected, in our unwanted, our hard, our confusing, and our unplanned—it's God handcrafting a path for us. Not overlooking or ignoring or punishing but, in fact, working hard with every little detail to be sure things will be even better than what we had in mind.

By continuously living His ways and being obedient, we'll find ourselves on the ride of our lives, a ride we were always intended to take. Times will come when we will feel at ease even among trials because from consistently trying to trust, we will experience time and time again that we are being led to the greater things. Times will come when the smiles are real, when the happiness is real, regardless of our situations. Times will come when the scary and the hard and the unexpected turn into exciting, thrilling, new adventures that come with peace and knowledge that we are in motion toward the best-fit blessings. And we'll be profoundly grateful that things didn't go our own way because we will find ourselves living our best self in our best life, living and experiencing things we didn't even know were available to us, because we chose to trust the most powerful Being to ever exist. And we'll wonder why we haven't done better all along.

Remembering God's purpose can prepare us for whatever is to come because whatever that may be, we'll know He is there. He is behind it. Which means all is not lost. It means we are not stuck, and we are not stagnant, and we are not sinking. It means we are not living linear. It means this is not final; we are not done. It means *things* can change and *we* can change.

It means good is always there because God is always there. And He does not sleep or take breaks. It means when it's out of our hands, it's in His. It means every passing second is a chance to turn it all around. It means we have a God of commas, not periods. It means regardless of our narrow vision for our life, *we are going somewhere* with all of this!

You may be in a hard season right now, but seasons don't last forever. Each one brings forth new blossoms. Never let a change of course take away from the unchangeable truth that God is taking care of you. Be obedient. Take heart in things not going how you wanted; take heart in your unexpected, in your hard, in your confusing and unplanned. It's God handcrafting a path for you. A better path. And you'll stand all amazed.

Are we allowing God to be God? *Embrace* the unexpected, knowing who is guiding you. Because He knows something we don't. Something greater.

Reach, JENEDY PAIGE

Christ and the Holy City, ROSE DATOC DALL

OBEDIENCE

Wherever He Leads Me

RON MILLBURN

I was working as an assistant to the area director in the seminary and institute program, and our offices were changing. We were moving to a beautiful new building, and I had the opportunity to choose a painting to put in my office. I picked out a beautiful painting by Greg Olsen and the FM group secured it to the wall. Soon after, the institute director came in and asked me if I had any Velcro. I reached into my drawer and gave him a roll and then asked him how he liked my new painting.

He looked at it for a moment and then said, "I don't like it very much."

That surprised me, so I asked him why.

He said, "I dunno. I just don't like it. Why do *you* like it?"

I said, "Well, it's got Jesus in it . . . and Jerusalem in the background."

"That's all? You know, unless a painting really speaks to you, unless it really *means* something to you, I don't think it should be hanging in your office. Does this painting speak to you?"

"Well, it's got Jesus in it . . ." I stammered.

"A lot of paintings have Jesus in them," he said and then walked away.

I sat there looking at the painting. It was beautiful, I thought, and it had Jesus in it and Jerusalem in the background, but I decided it wasn't really speaking to me.

I got up from my desk and walked over to the painting, then noticed the title at the bottom: "Wherever He Leads Me."

"What does that mean?" I asked myself. "Who is the 'He' and 'Me' in the painting?"

"In other words,
Jesus was saying He would go
wherever His Father wanted
Him to go and would do
whatever His Father wanted
Him to do."

I walked back to my desk, sat down, and just stared at the painting, pondering on the title: "Wherever He Leads Me."

Then, in an instant, the painting spoke to me. I don't know what Brother Olsen meant by the title, but from that moment on, and forever after, it would speak to me of Christ's complete, unwavering compliance to His Father's will. I filled in the pronouns in the title with, "Wherever Heavenly Father Leads Me, His Only Begotten Son." In other words, Jesus was saying He would go wherever His Father wanted Him to go and would do whatever His Father wanted Him to do. Even at age twelve, when Joseph and Mary searched three days and finally found Him teaching in the temple, Jesus said, "Why is it that ye sought me? Knew ye not that I must be about my Father's business?" (JST Luke 2:49).

Throughout His entire ministry, Jesus made it abundantly clear whose errand He was on. When His Apostles questioned whether He had eaten, He replied, "My meat is to do the will of him who sent me, and to finish his work" (John 4:34).

To the unbelieving Pharisees, Jesus said, "I seek not mine own will, but the will of the Father which hath sent me" (John 5:30).

To the people of Capernaum, Jesus declared, "For I came down from heaven, not to do mine own will, but the will of him that sent me" (John 6:38).

Later, the Savior testified, "He that sent me is with me: the Father hath not left me alone; for I do always those things that please him" (John 8:29).

As Jesus spent His last mortal hours with His Apostles, He told them, "I love the Father; and as the Father gave me commandment, even so I do" (John 14:31). Then He gave them this charge: "If ye keep my commandments, ye shall abide in my love; even as I have kept my Father's commandments, and abide in his love" (John 15:10).

And *there* is the key to His unwavering obedience: His love for the Father. And that is the key to our obedience. Jesus said, "If ye love me, keep my commandments" (John 14:15).

Love is a powerful action. When we love God, it motivates us to show Him our love through obedience. And when we are committed to that love, we are obedient even in times of great adversity.

"Wherever He Leads Me." I looked at the painting again. Jesus is standing on the Mount of Olives, and He's making a decision: go into Jerusalem or walk away. If He goes into Jerusalem, He will be "arrested and condemned on spurious charges, convicted to satisfy a mob, and sentenced to die on Calvary's cross" ("The Living Christ: The Testimony of the Apostles," *Ensign* or *Liahona*, Apr. 2000) He will be mocked, spit upon, humiliated, and scourged. He knows very well what He will be walking into if he goes down that path to Jerusalem. Does He go down, or does He walk away? The title tells the answer: "Wherever He Leads Me."

As I was pondering these things, the institute director walked in again. I said, "You know why this painting speaks to me?" I proceeded to tell him about the title and Jesus's decision to do the Father's will, even though Christ would be crucified. I quoted D&C 19:18, in which

Jesus describes His ordeal in Gethsemane: "Which suffering caused myself, even God, the greatest of all, to tremble because of pain, and to bleed at every pore, and to suffer both body and spirit—and would that I might not drink the bitter cup, and shrink—" I said, "Jesus never hesitated to do the Father's will—ever. He never asked to get out of anything the Father wanted Him to do—until Gethsemane. The suffering there was so intense, the anguish for our sins was so great that He bled from every pore. And for the first time in His mortal life, Jesus begged the Father for a reprieve: "Father, if thou be willing, remove this cup from me." He pleaded . . . but then added, "Nevertheless not my will, but thine be done" (Luke 22:42). And then Jesus forged ahead and drank that bitter cup, "the will of the Son being swallowed up in the will of the Father" (Mosiah 15:7).

Why did He do it? Not only because He loved us and wanted to save us from a physical and spiritual death but also because Jesus loved His Father. "Nevertheless," He said, "glory be to the Father, and I partook and finished my preparations unto the children of men" (D&C 19:19).

"So, that's what this painting means to me," I told the institute director with an emotion-filled voice that surprised me. "That's what it speaks to me."

He looked at me for a moment and then said, "Do you have any more Velcro?"

I gave him another roll, and he walked away.

I sat there thinking, What just happened? I pour out my soul about this painting, and the only comment he has is, "Do you have any more Velcro?"

A few minutes later, however, he poked his head around my door and said, "By the way, nice recovery."

More than a nice recovery, I thought. Though he was referring to me, I thought of the recovery that comes to all of us because Jesus followed that path down the Mount of Olives—the path He was foreordained to take—to drink, as He said, "out of that bitter cup which the Father hath given me, and have glorified the Father in taking upon me the sins of the world, in the which I have suffered the will of the Father in all things from the beginning" (3 Nephi 11:11).

Our recovery from a "lost and fallen state" was contingent on Jesus's walking down that path. And for our recovery to be complete, we also must walk down that path and prove that we are willing to "do all things whatsoever the Lord [our] God shall command [us]" (Abraham 3:25).

Not only does "Wherever He Leads Me" describe the unequivocal determination of Jesus to follow His Father, but by implication, it also describes our greatest mission and challenge in life: "Wherever He Leads Us."

ART CREDITS